ORGANIC GRIEF

A fresh, natural approach to healing after loss...

Lane Robinson, MBA

Cover photo of the Clark Fork River in Montana courtesy of Jeremy Oliver – JRo Photography

Photo of Lane Robinson by Tricia Muhlbauer, Personality Portraits

Library of Congress Cataloging-in-Publication Data

Robinson, Lane

Organic Grief – A fresh, natural approach to healing after loss... | Lane Robinson

ISBN 978-1701628892

Published in the United States of America

To Farah – with gratitude…

Contents

Introduction

Welcome to *Organic Grief*, a book that introduces a new
paradigm into the grieving journey by focusing on healing
the root causes of pain and suffering and not just treating
the symptoms. In Western society, there is no evidence-
based cure for grief. Sadly, most of the bereaved –
especially those in the US - get through the day by taking
mind-altering prescription drugs such as anti-depressants,
pain killers and sleeping pills. They also join grief groups
or work with therapists who often tell them that their
suffering will never end, that the general population
doesn't understand their grief, that grieving forever is
normal, and that they now have a safe place to suffer.

If you have been struggling on your healing journey after
trauma or loss and are looking for a better way, are ready
(even cautiously) to get your life back and move forward
from a position of optimism, and are able to accept that
suffering is neither productive nor required, then this
book is for you, my dear. It will debunk myths, explain
things that many people raised in the Western tradition
don't understand about death, dying and the other side,
and provide a roadmap for building a strong foundation
for your empowered healing journey.

I wrote this book after working as a professional medium
for ten years, a vocation that I didn't consciously choose,
and actually, attempted to avoid for many years. What I
eventually discovered was that Mediumship is a gift – and

one that must be shared as a fundamental healing modality. I also have learned much of what I share in this book from working with those who have lost loved ones, many suddenly or in agonizing ways – and from communicating with hundreds of departed souls. They are the real heroes of the stories we will share here.

This book is respectfully dedicated to a woman named Farah. She is a client whom I have never met. When I was going through the most challenging time of my life in 2016 and when I really didn't know if I was going to survive (you can read all about it in Chapter 11), Farah generously donated money to me and the only thing she wanted in return was for me to pay it forward. She believed in me and my work and was willing to help. Her donation enabled me to move to Santa Fe and start a healing practice here. I will never forget her generosity or the difference it has made. Her act of kindness literally saved my life, and I feel truly blessed.

Becoming a trauma expert has led me to experience a multitude of overwhelming challenges, any one of which could have and nearly did kill me. What they had in common is that they involved massive loss – a life-disabling brain injury, financial ruin, homelessness, the suicide of my young nephew, and finally the theft of 90% of my personal treasures and mementos of most of my memories - in a storage unit burglary. Every one of these things sucked majorly, and without my spirit team and my knowledge of how to heal using alternative therapies, I would probably be working as a spirit guide and thriving in bliss on the other side. But, I haven't yet finished my mission as an earthbound human.

However, as I look back on the trials that have been offered to me in my spiritual journey, I am now at peace and grateful for the wisdom that resulted from facing and overcoming each and every obstacle. Hopefully, sharing that wisdom with you will assist you profoundly in your own healing journey.

My intention is always to provide every client and student with unique, powerful, and extremely simple tools and information to help them transform their lives whether we are working together one-on-one over the telephone, in person in Santa Fe, New Mexico USA, or in a group setting.

If you enjoy and appreciate this book, then I encourage you to continue spending time with me by reading *"Enlightened by Accident – The Awakening of a Psychic Medium."* I wrote it to share my experience of transitioning from being a highly-respected international management consultant and the process I went through to become a metaphysical practitioner - and all of the crazy things that happened during that process. A few years later, I wrote another book called *"Stress Free Success – Where East Meets West!" Stress Free Success* explains the protocol I developed over nearly two decades to recover from what could have been a life-disabling injury. It is a great reference book and really does help to relieve anxiety and stress.

Thank you for purchasing this book and for taking the time to read and reflect on the information you will discover here. And, if you appreciate what you learned here, a positive review on Amazon would mean the world to me and help this book to help others to transform their healing journeys.

I'd love to connect with you and hear how your journey is going. You can check out my websites – laneknows.com showcases the services I provide as well as live events. Lightwalkerlife.com is an online resource center for those who have suffered overwhelming devastation or loss and provides blogs, online courses, and a team of incredibly talented healers who all work over the telephone to support our community of trauma survivors.

Everything happens for a reason and there is very important reason why you were drawn to this book. Regardless of whether you are dealing with the death of a loved one, recovering from a devastating event or natural disaster, coping with the loss of your job or a significant relationship, bouncing back from a traumatic physical injury or scary medical diagnosis – the information you will find here will help you gain new energy, a new perspective, and a renewed sense of strength. So, let's get started on our journey and make things work better – together.

Chapter 1

Loss is Like an Earthquake

"Death is life's change agent.
It clears out the old to make way for the new."
- Steve Jobs

Life and death happen. Most of the time we live each day comforted by predictable routines and satisfied by accomplishing the tasks of work and daily existence. But, sometimes we are just going through the motions, minding our own business, and seemingly out of nowhere, BAM! Something occurs that jolts us out of our comfort zone and makes us look at things completely differently. And even though we know these things can occur, and maybe even expect them; there's no way to prevent them, prepare for them, or escape from them.

Whether the disruptive event is a traumatic injury of ourselves or a loved one, a natural disaster, mass shooting, frightening medical diagnosis or death of a loved one – the results are the same; life as we know it is altered forever. Because traumatic situations occur without warning, are uncontrollable, tend to create physical and/or emotional damage, and are sometimes mind boggling; experiencing these events is kind of like being in a high magnitude earthquake.

If you have recently gone through one of these events, then you probably relate to this analogy. But, before we get into the nitty gritty about soul journeys and the process of dying and how to deal with a new reality after loss; I'd like to share a story about living in California and my naïve approach to earthquakes and how it resembles how many of us tend to think about preparing for loss. I'll never forget my first earthquake. I had just moved to Los Angeles to work for a boutique consulting firm owned by my friend and former boss. My objective was to learn how to run a consulting business so I could open my own independent practice someday.

I was sitting at my desk in a shared office, when suddenly, the floor underneath me started undulating in waves – and it felt as if I was on a boat. After three waves, the movement stopped. I'd only been in LA for a few weeks, and my colleagues started laughing at me, calling me an "earthquake virgin." I wasn't afraid, but had a difficult time wrapping my mind around the fact that the solid floor on which my desk sat had just moved in a seemingly impossible way.

These small, harmless earthquakes tend to freak out first timers, but Californians just shrug them off as commonplace. My teammates who were native to the Golden State actually joked that they used earthquakes under magnitudes of 4.5 to mix their margaritas. To them, seismic events were just a normal part of life.

But sometimes, earthquakes cause massive devastation. After nearly a year in LA, I moved to San Francisco to start my consulting practice. It was 1996, seven years after the horrific Loma Prieta earthquake that killed nearly 4,000 people and caused over five billion dollars in damage.[1] The image that haunted me was of the collapsed Oakland Bay Bridge – when the upper deck crumbled and crashed onto the lower deck, and I could just imagine what it would have been like to be driving a car over that bridge at the time of the quake. I've always been a little bit claustrophobic, and being crushed in my car in the middle of a bridge would be very low on my preferred list of ways to die (more on that later – because I believe there are some preferable ways to cross over when the time comes for each of us).

My love affair with San Francisco had started three years before, after I'd been sent there on a temporary assignment when I was doing internal marketing consulting for U S West, the phone company in Colorado. My friend Connie had moved from Denver to San Francisco a few years before and since she was the only person I knew who lived there, I sent her an email to let her know I'd be arriving soon to work on a project for the summer. I've always had good housing karma, and I hit the jackpot when I reached out to my friend.

She told me that it was a strange coincidence that I contacted her that day because she'd just found out about a really cool, fully-equipped flat that was available as a short-term rental in a sweet location in upper Pacific Heights. Not only was the neighborhood amazing, but it was just down the hill from the gates of the beautiful and historic Presidio National Park.

It turned out that close friends of Connie's owned a house in Tiburon, north of San Francisco across the Golden Gate Bridge, and they planned to live up there for several months and leave everything they owned in their flat in the city. They had just called Connie that morning to ask if she knew anyone who would like to stay in their place over the summer. And, as luck would have it - I would be the perfect person because I was dependable, honest, responsible, and a neat freak. This was in the days before AirBNB or VRBO and letting someone live in your home with all of your possessions in it was unheard of back then.

The flat was amazing. It was on the top floor of a vintage Victorian that was built after fire destroyed many homes in the city in 1906. It had views of Presidio Avenue out the front and views of the city and Saint Mary's Cathedral in the back from this huge bay window in the living room. It had a washer and dryer and two bathrooms (very rare) and the neighborhood was quiet and had great galleries a block away on Sacramento street and incredible restaurants like Garabaldi's (intimate dining for California and Mediterranean cuisine) right across the street and Ella's American Kitchen (famous for their chicken hash and cheesy polenta – gourmet comfort food) a couple of blocks away. Those restaurants are still there, by the way, and you should totally check them out if you visit San Francisco (breakfast at Ella's is unforgettable, but go on a weekday – on weekends the line starts forming at 7:30 AM).

Sorry, I'm a foodie and got distracted for a minute by fond food memories. But, let's get back to reminiscing about my dream flat. Staying there was win/win. My company didn't have to pay for a hotel, and I was able to experience the city by actually living there. The flat had a wicked awesome kitchen and I love to cook – so living in a hotel was always tricky for me.

The only catch was that I had kind of a crazy commute from the upper part of the city, across the Bay Bridge, to the Oakland suburb of Walnut Creek where our offices were. It was a forty-five minute, tension filled, white-knuckle experience each way, but I learned to suck it up and deal because I adored living in that flat so much.

But, every weekday, when I had to cross that bridge going to and from the office, I couldn't help but think about the Loma Prieta quake and visualize that image of the collapsed ruin in my mind's eye. Fortunately for me, no major quakes happened during that first summer. The project went well, and I returned to Colorado. But something about San Francisco kept calling to me as if I'd left a part of my soul there, and so I set a goal to go back and start my own consulting business someday.

As luck would have it, when I was ready to return, my old flat was available again. By now, the owners had moved all of their clothing and household goods to Tiburon and left most of the furniture and artwork in the flat. And, once again, they rented it to me at about 70% of its actual market value. I was overjoyed. This time, I mostly worked from home, but also had an office in the Financial District – a twenty minute bus ride away from my flat. For the first time in my life, I walked and rode public transportation everywhere and rarely drove my car. It was exciting to live in a real city and to experience it mainly by walking.

I moved to San Francisco because I loved the city. My love affair with the Golden Gate Bridge never waned, and the visual beauty of the city – the architecture and the views of the bay – brought me never-ending joy. On Saturday mornings, I would walk down Jackson Street and look at the exquisite homes behind wrought iron gates - on my way to the Lyon Street stairs located about three blocks from my flat at the intersection of Broadway and Lyon streets.

I'd take the stairs down to the bottom and walk a few blocks west through the picturesque Marina District past the Palace of Fine Arts and the St. Francis Yacht Club to the beachfront path that ended right under the magnificent Golden Gate bridge. On my way back to my flat, I'd stop at World Wrapps on Chestnut Street to grab a bean and cheese wrap and a Tropical Sun smoothie to enjoy at home.

I only knew a few people in the city. The teammates from my former consulting project mostly lived in the east bay or had traveled in just for the project as I did, so I didn't really have a support system and was mostly on my own. So, from the very first day I lived in San Francisco, I carried what I called earthquake insurance. The reason I called it insurance is because I figured that if I made sure I always had a few simple things with me, just in case, then no big earthquakes would happen.

You see, I'm one of those people who can't get away with anything. If I forget my wallet and drive a car, I will definitely be stopped by the traffic police. If I tell a white lie to someone about why I can't have dinner with them, then I will most certainly run into them that same evening. And, if I let my AAA subscription expire, then I'll have a flat tire. So, based on my previous life experience, I really believed that if I wasn't prepared for an earthquake – then the city was certain to be shaken up at some point in a big way during my time there.

This whole obsession with preparedness started for me at a very young age and has to do with the fact that I'm the oldest child, have Capricorn rising in my astrology (ruled by Saturn – the personal trainer of the Universe), and because I was raised in a strict household when the penalty for stupidity was steep.

So, for as long as I can remember, I've learned to do the right thing in order to avoid less than pleasant consequences, and I figured if I prepared for a big earthquake, then I could avoid being trapped by one. My portable earthquake kit consisted of a hundred dollars in cash, a liter of water, and shoes I could walk home in, and I took those things with me every time I left my flat. Every single time.

I figured out the thing about the shoes when I was taking a bus home from a meeting in the financial district one afternoon, and the bus broke down about 10 blocks from my flat on a street that was at least eight blocks away from a major bus route. The driver instructed us to get out of the bus and informed us that it could be hours before another bus arrived.

Sadly, I was wearing a suit with a pencil skirt and high heels and I'll never forget the long trudge home up and down the hills for which San Francisco is famous. After that experience, I switched from carrying a briefcase to a Coach backpack that had plenty of room for the shoes and the water. I lived and learned.

Fortunately, I never had to use that earthquake preparedness kit, but I did experience a few shaky quakes. In hindsight, while having those things with me made me feel better and more secure, in reality - if a devastating earthquake hit the city, then a fistful of cash, a bottle of water and some tennis shoes wouldn't have protected me.

Some life derailing events just happen and, like earthquakes there's no way to prepare for them. They come out of nowhere. They are unexpected. We can't control what happens to us before, during, or after they occur. We feel vulnerable. And, as soon as we get over the initial shock, the fear continues because with large earthquakes and emotionally overwhelming traumatic events, aftershocks can still happen.

Traumatic loss is like a destructive earthquake. It happens suddenly. Even though we knew all along that it could happen; when the actual event occurs – we realize we aren't prepared for it at all. And when that traumatic loss is caused by death, it especially rings true.

This phenomenon is what surprised me most about the death of my maternal grandmother, a person whom I adored with all my heart. Other than a friend who was killed in a car accident in middle school, the passing of my grandmother was my first experience with losing someone near and dear to me. And, even though we had anticipated her death for many years; when it happened, I felt like I'd been hit by a freight train. There is no way to prepare mentally or emotionally for the death of a loved one.

The bottom line is that if you are reading this, you know that you will certainly experience death in your lifetime including loss of family, friends, life partners, pets and acquaintances. All of us will also experience our own deaths. So, doesn't it make sense that we equip ourselves with the best information about death and dying?

Wouldn't it be helpful to know what happens during the process of actually crossing over? And, what if we could be assured that death is a natural part of life, and that it isn't something to be feared?

Would you like to have accurate information about where we actually end up after our lives on Earth end? Finally, what if we were able to choose to approach the grieving process from the perspective that grief is organic, natural, and creates opportunities for something new? Does that seem possible to you? And, if not, it is completely understandable; but you are probably reading this book because you are ready for a perspective shift and would like to learn more.

Sadly, for many of us who were raised in the Western tradition – death is something to be avoided and feared. We expect that it is final and signifies an ending. We've been taught that the death of a child, friend, family member, life partner or any other loved one is a tragic and devastating event from which those of us who survive will never recover. And the cause of someone's death whether it was due to a long illness, a medical error, a sudden accident, a shooting, or a natural disaster makes it even worse.

Finally, if the person crossed over at a young age, then that adds to the burden of grief and makes the loss even more debilitating for survivors. So many people are walking around today carrying a monumental grief burden, and have allowed that grief to play a starring role in their life stories. But, while loss is part of the story of every human at some point, it doesn't have to be the theme.

While we've grown up believing that the only justified death happens when an elderly person dies while sleeping and that all other death is horrid and wrong, then we're setting ourselves up to endure many years of misery. It is interesting that after someone dies, most of us focus on what we lost, and on the end of the relationship and the finality of it all. But, if death is like an earthquake, then why don't we respond to it in the same way? Typically, after earthquakes people tend to focus on working together to build new, stronger, better, and more resilient buildings, instead of struggling to survive day-to-day in the rubble.

So, as we progress through this book – we will provide some real and true information about death and dying to assist you so you can ease your pain and suffering and reframe your loss within a new context. Then, in the second half of the book, we will offer simple, effective and practical tools for you. The intention is to support you so that you can create a new, stronger, better and more resilient formula for living after loss and moving forward on your healing journey.

Chapter 2

Myths versus Reality

"To the well-organized mind, death is but the next great adventure."

- J. K. Rowling

Most people of my generation - who grew up during the last half of the 20th century, were taught that death was something to be feared, and that it was morbid and horrible. But, for my grandparents, death was a natural part of life. Many of their generation lived on farms and raised animals for meat. Medical epidemics, limited access to doctors, ineffective birth control, and living without the modern comforts we take for granted today all contributed to shorter life spans.

My grandmother was one of thirteen children and lost half of her siblings (six brothers and sisters) during the scarlet fever epidemic in the early 1900's. Her older brother died in a farming accident several years later. She experienced death first hand, and up close from the time she was a small child.

At the turn of the 20th century, people had minimal access to funeral services and so communities took care of the dead on their own. In my grandparents' day, it was perfectly normal and even expected that when someone died, the women in the family would clean and clothe the body, and then it would be laid out on the dining room table or in a casket in the parlor. Then, the family would open up their home for visitation so that everyone could pay their respects before the burial. It wasn't weird, or strange, or creepy. It was normal, and even though it was sad and often difficult, death was out in the open and accepted as a reality of life.

But, my parents, on the other hand, whispered about death and tried to shelter their kids from it. But, that wasn't surprising because their entire generation was rooted in escapism. I think it was partially because they grew up during the Great Depression and World War II and people of their generation just wanted to have fun and forget the harsh realities of their childhoods.

I can understand that being a kid during a time when economic disaster, the horrors of the holocaust, having air raid drills at your elementary school, and seeing bombings of European cities on the newsreels at the movie theater created bleak viewpoints. However, I'm not sure that the escapism and the complete shift in lifestyles during the 1950's and 1960's make complete sense.

The TV series Mad Men really illustrates what it was like when my parents were young adults with little kids – they consumed cocktails at all hours of the day. Smoking cigarettes was considered cool and sophisticated, and they smoked incessantly, even at the dinner table. And from the perspective of their generation, parents were the center of the Universe and for them and many of their peers, kids were unavoidable nuisances.

When my parents reached adulthood, the concept of suburbs was created, offering a new type of community that provided an alternative to urban or rural living. The homes on the edges of cities were large enough to allow kids to have separate bedrooms and the parents to enjoy more privacy. Living in a suburb gave kids the freedom to get out of the house and spend time in the neighborhood. While we were still actively engaged with our families; we were separated from our parents and siblings more than previous generations were.

So, it is no surprise that my first awareness of death, and it was really awareness – knowledge that someone I knew could die and that death actually happens, first appeared in my world cloaked in secrecy, controversy, and shadow. I was ten years old. It all started when my grandmother asked my mother if my two sisters (ages eight and six) and I could visit my grandparents' cabin in the mountains for the weekend.

It was springtime and that meant that it was time to open up the cabin for summer. My grandmother really wanted us to go because the cabin was the happy place for all of us. We enjoyed every minute there, whether trapping chipmunks in homemade cages, filling up the bird feeders, or simply breathing the fresh, pine scented air. We had been going there since I was five, and it was my very favorite place.

My grandparents' cabin was located in Coal Creek Canyon about an hour west of Denver, Colorado. My grandfather, who became a general contractor after WWII, built it himself. In the beginning, it didn't have electricity or running water. It was SO cool. My grandmother would pump water by hand from the kitchen sink.

She cooked on a cast-iron wood stove and moved the burners around to control the heat. Watching her cook was like watching an orchestra conductor leading a symphony. There was an elegance of motion and timing and energy, and my grandmother was a true master of her art form. You could taste the love in the meals she created.

Even though the cabin didn't have modern conveniences, it was completely equipped for comfort. There was a white, metal and enamel urn with a lid that had a cut out for hanging a ladle for drinking water. We took baths in a trough-like tub in the kitchen near the stove.

We would go in pairs to the outhouse that was a two seater because there were cougars and bears in the woods and little kids couldn't go out there alone. It was painted pink inside and we called it the Pink Pearl. A few years later, the cabin got plumbing and an indoor bathroom, but I loved it the most when we learned from my grandmother to live as the pioneers did.

At the cabin, we played hide and seek in the wardrobe in the entry way, or behind the curtain that covered up the wood storage alcove where my grandmother got her kindling for the stove. Since there was no TV, we played Chinese checkers and cards for hours on end, and I got to sleep with my skinny sisters in a huge four poster bed with a fluffy down comforter. It was my definition of heaven on earth.

My mom would drop us off at my grandparents' house in Denver about an hour away from where we lived. And then we would pack up my grandfather's big maroon Pontiac sedan and he would drive us all to the cabin. My grandmother didn't drive, so we all depended on Grandpa whenever traveling in a car was required. So, when I heard my mom talking on the phone about me and my sisters going to the cabin the next weekend, I couldn't wait to go.

Normally, my parents loved handing us off to our grandparents to get us out of their hair. But this time was different because my grandfather's health had begun to decline and even though my mother wasn't that concerned, the final decision about anything that required permission and my mother's parents always belonged to my dad.

I remember my parents' heated conversation in which my dad expressed his concern about my grandfather dying when we were visiting. His reasoning was completely fear based. I can still hear my dad ranting. What if he dies in front of the kids? What if he dies when he is driving and the kids are in the car? How messed up would it be if the kids saw him die or saw their grandmother break down?

My mom actually thought it would be helpful to my grandparents to spend time with us. In the end, though, my dad made the decision and it wasn't open for debate. We weren't going. The really tragic part was that my grandfather passed away several months later, and we never went back to the cabin again. My parents didn't want anything to do with it, and so my grandmother sold it later that year.

It was heartbreaking for me because it was my personal sanctuary. To this day, I still cherish those memories and re-live the joy I felt during those special summers at the cabin. Now that I have the freedom to live my bliss, my house in the foothills is my sanctuary. My grandmother taught me a love for pine-scented air, wildlife, and the peace that comes from being surrounded by a forest.

My grandfather, Oren S. Blennerhassett (nicknamed Blue because he was a subdued and introspective person), was a decorated war hero who survived the attacks on Pearl Harbor when he was a Master Sergeant in the Army Air Corps (Air Force) at Wheeler Field in Hawaii. During his tenure on Oahu, he began to have lung issues from the humid ocean air, and soon after the Pearl Harbor attacks, he was re-assigned to Lowry Field in Denver to become the assistant to the General there.

My grandfather was not a very large person – he was built kind of like the actor Robert Redford, 5'6" and lean. But he was wickedly handsome and had a sparkle in his eye. He and my grandmother were soul mates. She ran the household and when he wasn't tinkering in the garage or remodeling or repairing something around the house, he sat in his chair and smoked a pipe. Even though he was physically strong enough to build a cabin by himself, his health and vitality fluctuated after middle age.

He passed away at the age of 63 from a heart attack while eating a piece of pie at a diner in his hometown of Leavenworth, Kansas. I remember when my mother got the phone call. An only child, she had always been closest to her dad. The funeral was going to be in Kansas because my grandfather was going to be buried with honors at Fort Leavenworth, and so my mom had to scramble to pack and go.

I wanted to be there to support my mom and my grandmother (even at a young age, I felt protective of others and had a healer instinct), but my parents let me know in no uncertain terms that a funeral was no place for a child and that there was no way that I was going. My mom kept trying to not cry in front of us kids and the whole experience made me feel queasy.

My mom's parents had not been enthusiastic about her marrying my dad, and so there was always friction there. It wasn't surprising that my dad didn't attend the funeral either. Since my dad worked full time, and wasn't able to take care of us on his own, his mother came to stay with us. She felt uncomfortable because she was never the favorite grandmother and she was afraid of felines, so every time our cat came into the room, she freaked out.

The whole experience was unsettling and made me feel scared and insecure. In our household, as far as my parents were concerned, kids didn't have rights and our primary job was to do as we were told. There was no point in me trying to make my case for attending the funeral.

When my grandmother returned from Kansas, she was extremely sad, but she was proud of my grandfather's military honors funeral. She showed us the photos afterwards, and my parents were mortified that we saw pictures of my grandfather's body in the open casket. My youngest sister had nightmares for years after seeing those funeral pictures. The pictures didn't freak me out, but they made me feel really sad for my grandmother's loss.

But, my parents' attitudes about the whole situation – from the time when my grandfather first became ill, to the funeral, and their reactions to conversations we had with our grandmother afterwards, just added to my fear surrounding the topic of death. I learned then that when someone dies, the whole situation is all about darkness, and keeping a stiff upper lip, and shielding the reality – especially from the kids.

But my grandmother had a different attitude. When we were looking at the funeral pictures, we had a conversation about death. And, she even explained to me what happens when people die – at least ten years before anyone ever wrote a book about having a near death experience. At the time, I didn't realize that my grandmother actually had the ability to communicate with the departed. I just thought she told really good ghost stories!

She explained that death wasn't anything to be feared because our departed family members would be there to assist us and welcome us to the other side. She also described the tunnel of loving light that we would all pass through. She knew all about it a full ten years before anyone wrote a book about near death experiences.

I wondered at the time how she could be so certain about this, but she spoke with such conviction that I believed her completely. Later, I realized that she had communicated with departed friends and family members, and that they had shared the information with her. My grandmother even explained to me that she actually spoke with her departed siblings soon after they passed. She described seeing them gathered at the end of her bed, just above the foot rail.

When my grandfather died, she also talked to him all the time as if it were completely normal and told me that she could see him in her bedroom at night. When I discovered my abilities as a medium, it finally made sense to me that I inherited these gifts from my grandmother and that everything she had explained to me was true.

It really isn't our fault, that, as Americans, most of us have been grossly misinformed about death. I believed all of the morbid myths just like everyone else, until I realized my gifts as a medium in middle age. And then, everything changed because I was able to question friends and family members on the other side and obtain the information first hand.

Learning the truth has been life changing for me. I don't fear death. To me, it isn't weird or creepy or scary. It is actually a huge relief to have a whole new perspective. So, one of the main purposes of this book is to share the messages that death, dying and grieving are organic – natural, and fundamental to being human. In order to approach these subjects appropriately, we need to discover new information.

Have you been raised to fear dying? Do you wonder if there's life after death? Are you carrying guilt about what you did or didn't do before, during, or after a loved one crossed over? How would you feel if you knew that death is a natural part of the circle of life and that it is easy, and that all souls live on in spirit? If you read this book, then this is entirely possible and you will also learn how to navigate a new course during your grieving journeys – for the rest of your life.

I hope that you will keep an open mind and an open heart during this examination process because understanding the facts can lift a huge burden from your life. I'm going to briefly talk about the myths that I had been taught were true, and then in the next several chapters, we will dig deeper and I'll share stories about how my beliefs have changed and why, so you can understand what I experienced to validate a new perspective.

First of all, most of us have been taught that the process of dying is painful and scary and horrible. Based on what I've learned from the departed, most of the time, this is simply not true. When the body is in the final stages of dying, the person often experiences relief and joy. I wonder if it is just fear of the unknown that causes us to be apprehensive about the whole thing.

Many of us also wonder if death is final, and are concerned that we only live once and when it's over, it's over. In my experience, the soul lives on after the body dies and mainly does so because of quantum physics. The soul crosses over and settles in, and then assumes responsibilities on the other side until it becomes a permanent spirit guide or reincarnates.

So many people feel guilty about causing the death of a loved one or not being able to prevent it. In my experience, and this was a huge revelation for me – the soul decides when it will cross over and no human can prevent that from happening. And, as difficult as it is to accept, even when someone dies from apparent negligence or violence; the soul decided to be present in circumstances that would cause death. People don't die because they are in the wrong place at the wrong time. When a person dies, it is never anyone's fault. We'll go into this in quite a bit of detail later and share stories about real people who crossed over and how we know that the timing was soul driven.

If we accept that whenever someone dies, the soul decides, then we are able to rethink the whole concept of the tragedy of dying young. When a soul departs after a limited time on the planet, I believe it is because that soul has completed its mission in being present during the journeys of friends and family. And, contrary to what most of us have been taught, we never die alone. We are accompanied by different energies from the spirit realm, and we'll explain who they are and how it all works.

In many Western families, people believe that they have a responsibility to be present at the time of death, especially when there is the opportunity to do so in a hospital, hospice or at home. Interestingly, most of the departed spirits with whom I've conversed have told me that they purposely crossed over when no people were there in the room with them. We'll share some stories about this and explain why this happens so frequently.

When children die, in particular, the parents feel that it is the most tragic thing that could ever happen. They feel guilty. And they are often angry that they have been robbed of a future with their children. The notion that parents' jobs are to ensure the safety of their children and that they are capable of doing so is also kind of an illusion. When the soul decides to leave, there is always a reason and that reason may or may not be evident to those of us who remain.

Later in the book, I'm going to share for the first time ever the conversation I had with my nephew Eric, who took his own life at the age of 27. As difficult as this information is to share, I feel responsible to do so to dispel the myths I used to have about suicide and the death of young people.

Another reason that many people fear dying is that they are afraid of going to hell. I believe that all souls go to the same place after the body dies, but they experience different things. We'll talk about the whole assimilation process, how it works, what happens, and why - and also what occurs when a soul is fully integrated on the other side. And, we'll explain how our loved ones stay connected to us and how we can communicate with them.

We've also not been fully educated about how to honor the departed. Most of the time, they are present and aware of what happens at their funerals and memorial services. Also, they often stay connected to family and friends and even visit from time to time. However, over time, they release attachment to events including what happens during their celebrations of life, and also to possessions including clothing, furniture and homes. It is important to understand what the departed care about and what we are able to let go of as survivors during our healing journeys.

The final myth we will confront, and this may be the most important one - has to do with mourning the loss of those we love. Most people I know (who aren't mediums) believe that the amount of pain and suffering they experience after someone dies is an indication of how much they loved that person. So, it is our social norm that if we love someone deeply, it is our duty to be sad, to feel devastated, and to accept the fact that we will not move on, never love again, and that we should feel guilty whenever we feel happy or joyful. And, for some reason we think that all of these things honor the memory of our person.

But the truth is that departed loved ones do not want survivors to suffer. When we allow the loss of a loved one to assume a starring role in our life stories, it is actually tragic. We'll share some stories later about medium readings I've done and explain why this is true and so important to understand.

And, debunking all of the myths we've been taught to believe about death and dying and the other side wouldn't be complete if we didn't understand what happens to survivors after someone dies – physically, emotionally and energetically and share information about the organic way to heal from loss and move on. Because, in the Western tradition; there is no evidence-based cure for grief. In other words, traditional medicine offers prescription drugs and psychotherapy to the bereaved, but the truth is that there is no proof that either of these remedies provides cures for grief.

So, we will devote the second half of this book to exploring what does work and explaining how you can make small, simple changes in your life and obtain access to therapies that ease pain and suffering during the grieving journey. We will also explain why pain and suffering are actually not required and something we can choose or not after a loved one crosses over. Suffering doesn't heal. It depletes the body, mind and spirit and contrary to popular belief, does not honor the departed.

Are you still with me? As an experienced medium, I know for sure that every single one of the things we just introduced as Western myths are widely held beliefs and that they don't tell the whole story. So, in the next several chapters, I will do my best to address each one of them and explain how I obtained the information. Then we will explore how we can all use this new knowledge to improve our lives and our perceptions about death – and move forward without fear for the rest of our lives.

Chapter 3

Soul Journey Fundamentals

*"You don't have a soul. You are a soul.
You have a body."*

- C.S. Lewis

Before we attempt to present new information about each
of the myths that many of us have been taught about
death, dying and grieving, it is important to agree on
some basic fundamentals. Let's start by defining the soul.

According to the Merriam-Webster dictionary, the soul is
defined as "the immaterial essence, animating principle,
or actuating cause of an individual life."[2]

I would edit this slightly and say that the soul is
"Encapsulated cosmic energy that inhabits a physical

vessel to create life." Let me explain. So, the soul is that thing that provides the life force energy within us. When we are alive as humans, the soul is grounded within the body. At the moment of death, the soul in its encapsulated form, leaves the body completely and returns to the place in the cosmos that is often referred to as "the other side of the veil."

Before I was a medium, I received validation about the concept of the soul as life-giving vital force energy. It happened when I saw my first dead person. Sadly, that person was my beloved maternal grandmother, Grace. She passed away when I was in my twenties, and before a traumatic brain injury literally changed my mind, I was a rock - the person whom everyone counted on in an emergency. Before the age of forty, I probably only cried five times in my life. So, I guess it wasn't surprising that when my grandmother went into the hospital for the last time, my mother and sister turned to me for support.

The prelude to my grandmother's death happened for me when I arrived at Denver's Stapleton Airport after a business trip to unexpectedly find my mother and my youngest sister at the gate waiting for me when I got off of the airplane. This was before mobile phones and airport security rules and people would actually go to the gate to meet arriving friends and family members. But I hadn't arranged for them to pick me up, and it wasn't normal for them to do that, and so it didn't make sense to me that they were there.

They explained that my grandmother was in the ICU and wasn't expected to live much longer. Since I had left a car at the airport, I decided to drive directly to the hospital. My mom and sister had been there all day, so I told them it was perfectly fine for me to go by myself.

My grandmother was at Fitzsimmons Army Medical Center. Even though I had been preparing for my grandmother's passing for years, it was a shock to see her in the hospital bed. It was like that unexpected earthquake that comes out of nowhere and while you're experiencing the shaking of the earth, you're still in denial. Even though I knew that my grandmother was 91 years old, had suffered with arthritis pain and the loss of my grandfather, and that she was the last survivor of all of her friends and family members, admitting that it was her time to go was still excruciating for me.

When I went into the room, she had a ventilator plugged into her throat to help her breathe, so she couldn't talk to me. She had the brightest blue eyes and as I spoke to her, I could see the light in them. Especially at the end of her life, she was very religious. So, I told her that it was ok for her to cross over and said a prayer asking Jesus to escort her through the tunnel of light. I was shattered, but tried to keep a stiff upper lip and not do the ugly cry in front of her. I kissed her on the forehead and then left the hospital with tears pouring down my face.

I needed to find peace, and so I drove to the chapel at Saint John's Cathedral where I attended church and got down on my knees and prayed. I didn't feel comforted, but at least I was able to hold it together driving to my home in Washington Park just a few minutes away. I fell into bed feeling overwhelmed and exhausted. This entire situation had come out of nowhere and was out of my control.

I learned the next morning that my grandmother passed away a few hours after I left the night before. I think she had been waiting to see me one last time. Several days later, I went to the funeral home to see her body. For some reason, I was alone there too. I remember that one of the people who worked at the funeral home opened the door to the viewing room. He stood at the doorway when I went in. I looked into the casket and saw a person that I didn't recognize. I told him. "This must be the wrong room because this is not my grandmother." He said, "She looks lovely." Ok, he was kind of creepy, but strange as it sounded; it was what I needed to hear at the time.

And, then I looked at her hands and the reality hit me. She had really distinct finger nails – strong and polished and filed to a point. And I had to accept the fact that this was my grandmother, even though the shell of a woman lying in front of me did not resemble her in any way. Her soul was so bright that when it left her body, her entire essence left also. And this is when I understood the concept of the soul providing vital force energy to the body.

Have you had a similar experience when seeing a dead person? Most of the time, a dead body closely resembles the person when they were alive, except that the individual appears to be sleeping. But, every once in a while a person like my grandmother dies, and their body doesn't resemble them at all afterwards because it was merely a shell that housed a great big bundle of bright spiritual energy.

This whole concept of certain souls radiating big light and bright energy was validated for me when I started training as a medium. I'm going to digress a little bit here and get into quite a bit of detail about what it is like to train as a medium before I explain the bright soul thing, because I think that it will help you to understand an insider's perspective about this unusual calling.

Mediumship training is unlike anything else I've ever experienced. It can be magical, and fun and also very stressful for novice mediums. Mediumship is a tricky process and we all want to do the best job we can, but at the end of the day, it isn't really about us individual mediums at all. Mediumship requires the biggest leap of faith, because in reality, we are vessels through which spirit works.

Ideally, mediumship training is both cerebral and experiential. The cerebral part consists of attending lectures about how Mediumship works and learning how to develop a process for receiving messages. The experiential part is based on giving and receiving Medium readings.

In the beginning, it is terrifying; but eventually, those of us who work professionally move through the fear and learn to completely trust spirit and just let it all work. What is also really cool about training as a medium is the ability to observe how other mediums operate, and how differently we approach the work based on our own gifts and philosophies.

I was lucky to train with some of the top teachers and alongside some of the most amazing students in the world. I learned by doing readings one-on-one, in front of small groups (4 to 8 people) on stage in front of my classmates, and finally on stage in front of a large group (150 people) of volunteers from the general public.

One of the most interesting things I learned during training is that all of us mediums can connect with the departed and receive messages. We do that in our own unique ways. Being able receive information from the departed by definition makes someone a medium. But surprisingly, connecting and receiving messages aren't the most important elements of the gift.

What separates a good medium from a great medium is the way in which he or she communicates the information and delivers messages. This is the thing I really learned to focus on and make part of my intention when working as a medium. My objective is to deliver messages respectfully and with compassion; and to articulate what the departed loved one is communicating - accurately and in a manner that is accessible and memorable for the recipient. Not all mediums do this, but in my experience, the great ones rock at it.

When I started training as a medium, I had never had a Mediumship reading and I didn't even know any mediums. So, in class when we did practice readings; I would always ask my fellow student mediums to communicate with my grandmother. She was my favorite person on the other side, and to be honest, I only knew a handful of dead people.

My family of origin is really small. My parents were both only children, and I have two sisters. We didn't have aunts or uncles or cousins. My father was estranged from his family and my mom's parents were older when they had her, so by the time we were born, most of those distant relatives were dead.

So, whenever I was in a medium training class, I would ask for a message from my grandmother. And most of the time, the medium who was attempting to connect with her would say that the pink light radiating from her spirit was so bright and pervasive that they weren't able to get past it to connect with and receive messages from her.

I will be forever grateful to a very talented medium named Maria, the only one who has ever been able to actually see through the brilliant light of my grandmother's spirit and deliver messages from her to me. The good news is that Maria made a strong connection with my grandmother and the messages I received that day were specific, accurate and validating. And like most good medium readings, they were life-changing and tremendous gifts for me.

Today I know that the color pink is an expression of love and pink light is actually used by many metaphysical healers to protect ourselves from absorbing the energy of clients. My grandmother, unbeknownst to me when she was alive, was (and still is) one bad ass spiritual being. I have a feeling she is radiating pink light because she is working with and helping other souls to heal from some challenging situations on the other side.

Now that we've talked about the concept of the soul, and if we acknowledge that all living beings have souls, then the question becomes – how are souls created? I'm not sure what motivates a soul to incarnate, but I do think that during the process a portion of cosmic energy is encapsulated in a silver net. I actually see it as a bubble. And the type and mixture of that energy informs the soul's personality.

After a soul is formed, it is called to inhabit a vessel for the first time. The location of the first lifetime informs the soul's values. You can read all about this in my book "Stress Free Success" where I go into this in great detail, but for now, let's just agree that these encapsulated bubbles of energy with unique characteristics (souls) are floating around in the Universe on the other side of the veil. And let's also accept that these souls form groups with other souls and interact with each other. And to take it a step further, let's assume that anyone who is in your family of origin is a part of your same soul group.

Soul groups exist to assist souls in evolving and gaining wisdom. They also assist souls before they incarnate into physical vessels and when they return to the other side. So this is consistent with my grandmother's explanation that when we die, our ancestors will be there to welcome us to the other side.

Death is not final and it is not the end. Souls exit the body and return to the other side where they live on energetically. This is true for humans and animals. As a medium, during readings with clients, I've frequently seen pets sitting next to departed loved ones on the other side.

And, even though I'm not an animal medium, whenever a close friend tells me that their dog or cat died; I can see the animal and describe it to them.

I've also learned that souls have personalities because whenever I do medium readings, I can feel the energy of the departed person and if they were funny and talkative in life, then that is a bonus because they will just start communicating with me. But if they were silent and unobtrusive in life, it can sometimes be challenging to get them to open up and share messages.

The other thing that I find to be amazing every single time it happens is when souls share information with me using phrases they used with their friends and family members. Whenever I repeat phrases like "It is what it is," or "Don't cry for me Argentina," or "Life is like a box of chocolates," or "Don't worry be happy," or other phrases frequently used by the departed, it conveys the message that the soul is near, happy, and still connected to their loved ones who remain.

At this point, I'm feeling like I should share a story about something that actually happened to me. It is relevant now because it addresses the question about whether or not Mediumship is real.

I was living in the mountains of Colorado, near a town called Woodland Park. Woodland Park is a darling village, located at the base of Pikes Peak about an hour west of Colorado Springs. One of my favorite places in Woodland is the Studio West Aveda Day Spa. I went there to get my hair styled, and on this particular day, I had this amazing woman named Melissa do my makeup. I was preparing to travel to Los Angeles and train to give medium readings on stage, and I knew that makeup is really important because it helps the audience members see facial expressions.

So, when I came out into the waiting area of the salon, after having my makeup done, the owner told me how great I looked. And, there was a woman waiting for her appointment, and she asked me why I had splurged on getting makeup done. And, I explained that I was a psychic medium and that I was preparing to go to a class to learn how to give readings on stage.

And, her response blew me away. She said, "So, you basically are a liar and a fake and you are going to learn how to give generic information to poor, unsuspecting people in the audience?"

For a second, I just stood there in total shock. And, before I tell you how I responded, I need to share some information with you. If you meet me in person, I'm one of those people who looks totally reliable and dependable. I'm that woman who people ask for help in retail stores because they think I work there, even though I don't. One time, I was in London outside the gates of Saint James' Park and three people asked me for directions. One was American. One was French, and I answered her in French. The other person was British but lived in the countryside. And, I was able to answer all of their questions!

So, me being my normal, regular, responsible self; I said to her. "Look at me. Do you think I look like a liar, a deceiver, and a fraud? Most people don't understand this, and neither did I until I discovered my gifts in middle age, but Mediumship is completely real, not phony, not made up, and is actually a healing modality. Have you ever had a reading?" She turned her nose up and said, "No, I think it is the work of the devil."

And, at that point, I just shook my head and walked to the door. Because, after living as a medium for ten years, I have accepted the fact that some people just don't want to understand the work we do and why we do it, and we can talk until we are blue in the face and they won't get it.

Have you ever wondered if Mediumship is real? Have you seen the television shows where they have a psychic medium as one of the characters in a specific episode and everyone jokes about it and wonders if they are real? Would it make sense to you if I told you that I actually avoided using my gifts as a medical intuitive, medium and healer because I didn't want my consulting clients to think I was a freak? Also, if none of these metaphysical gifts were real – why would someone like me give up a highly paying career as a well-respected consultant and all of the sudden turn into a fake gypsy fortune teller?

We're going to explain much more about this later. All I can say is that even though a small number of mediums like to do the "ghost buster" thing and make people think that Mediumship is creepy and dark, most of us work on the light side of the Force. I actually work with an entire team including a handful of Archangels and even Jesus and Mother Mary.

Oh, yes, I'm a baptized Christian (at the age of 28) and am very closely connected with Jesus and am grateful he introduced me to his mother because she is a phenomenal healer and pain reliever. I'll share more about that later. And, after doing so many readings I can't count them all, I've never had a weird, scary, or dark experience when working as a medium. That's the truth!

So, let's summarize. Isn't it fascinating to know that souls live on after death, on the other side of the veil until they reincarnate? And, isn't it also cool that they retain the same personalities they had during their lifetimes? Finally, isn't it magical that mediums can connect with the departed and share information in the same way that the departed loved one would have phrased it? This is the honest truth.

Now seems like a good time to talk about how souls actually travel to the other side and the process the soul goes through in leaving the body and integrating back into the cosmos. It's time to examine what happens when we die. And we will do that in the next chapter. We'll also talk about some misconceptions most survivors have about their responsibilities during and after someone dies.

Chapter 4

Traveling to the Other Side

"Dying is the easiest thing you'll ever do in your life."

- Message to Lane from a woman named Kate

Even though being a medium definitely has its ups and downs, one of the most majorly cool things about it is being able to have actual conversations with the departed and to understand what they experienced when they died – how they felt, what happened, and what their existence is like on the other side.

I'll never forget the medium reading in which the quote above was delivered to me. I was a novice medium and this particular situation was so unique. I share this story with my client's permission. My client was a woman named Ann. Ann's husband, Rob sadly passed away in his early fifties. Before the reading, I learned that when Ann was getting out of the car at Rob's funeral, her cell phone rang and she was told that her two sisters had been in an automobile accident on the way to the funeral, and that one of her sisters had died.

When I heard this story, I was blown away. Can you imagine learning at your spouse's funeral that your sibling was killed in a car accident on the way there? It was one of those readings that could have been mired in deep sorrow and lots of tears. But, surprisingly, it wasn't that way at all. You see, Ann's sister Kate, the driver of the car, was the sibling who died. And Kate was, in a word, hilarious!

During the reading I could see the accident and I knew that Kate had been driving and that she had died instantly at the scene. Kate told me that dying was "a walk in the park. It was a piece of cake." She then said that "dying is the easiest thing you'll ever do in your life." These words really took me by surprise.

Kate explained that she never knew what hit her. It turned out that a tire blew out and she lost control of the car and it veered off the road and hit a massive tree head on. Even though it would seem that she died in excruciating pain from the injuries she sustained during the crash, Kate explained that she didn't suffer. She was alive for a short time after the impact. She remembered that her whole body felt numb as if it was in shock.

And then she told me that "the most beautiful thing happened." She could see a bright light approaching her.

She remembered being drawn into the light and when her body was surrounded, she felt warm and safe and completely secure. And then she saw angels on the sides of the tunnel of light hovering next to her and lifting her up. She began to travel upwards through the tunnel of light as if she was flying.

At some point, she remembered looking down at the car and seeing her sister there and realizing that her sister was alive and would be ok. And, as much as you would expect that Kate would feel sad, she felt fine because she had begun to separate from the whole human experience and was embarking on a whole new adventure.

During the reading, she wanted me to emphasize to both of her sisters that she felt no pain after the crash. She wanted them to know that she didn't suffer at all. She didn't die alone, but was accompanied by celestial spirits and felt completely comforted and safe. The process of dying wasn't scary. It wasn't dark or creepy or weird. It was incredible.

Here's some more information that dispels two of our myths from Western society. We don't need to fear death. And, no matter how many people are with us or not with us when our souls leave our bodies, no one dies alone. All humans are accompanied by angels and spirit guides during the transition to the other side. And, according to my grandmother Grace, our ancestors and departed pets are there to greet us when we arrive on the other side.

The other thing that is interesting about Kate's situation was that her body was severely injured as a result of the car crash. Ann told me during the reading that she was worried that Kate had suffered because they literally had to cut her body out of the car. And, one of the things that was so interesting for me was that Kate was laughing and positive and didn't remember her death as being traumatic, nor scary, nor painful. Even though, based on how she died, we would naturally assume that it would have been horrible.

I believe that even when people's bodies die in hideous ways, even when there is violence and bloodshed and horrific emotional trauma, the spirit takes over very early on in the process; and as soon as that soul enters the light, a kind of energetic shock takes over the body and numbs the sensations of physical pain and struggle. Kate isn't the only one to have shared this same kind of story with me and I'll share some more stories later.

Numerous books have been written on the subject of near-death experiences (NDE) and two of my favorites are "Dying to Be Me,"[3] by Anita Moorjani; and "Proof of Heaven,"[4] by Dr. Eben Alexander. If you are interested in this subject, then I encourage you to read their stories and eliminate any fear or apprehension you might have had about the process of dying. You can also search for other books and articles that have been written on this topic. Now is a great time to release that burden of believing that death is terrifying and final.

I've also learned from doing readings and through my own personal training in working with Archangels, that Archangel Azrael is often present when souls cross over and that you can ask that he accompany your loved ones to the other side when you believe that their deaths are imminent. Azrael brings a quiet strength and tremendous comfort during the process of journeying to the other side. As an Archangel, he is by definition an assistant to God and he is able to assist an infinite number of people at a time.

And now, let's look at another myth – that it is best if surviving loved ones are there at their person's bedside at the time of death. I know that this one isn't true because it is one of the most frequent topics that arises during medium readings. It starts when the surviving person apologizes to the departed person for not being there at the time of their death. And most of the time, the departed person explains that they were relieved that no one was there. And the surviving person is almost always shocked because they have been carrying the guilt and remorse forever.

I've heard so many survivors tell the same story, and it goes like this. The relatives all flew in because someone was expected to die very soon. Everyone took turns spending time with the person who was dying, and the family was committed to always having someone there so that their loved one wouldn't die alone.

And then, finally after a few days of round-the-clock vigils, the family decided to just take a break and go out to dinner together. And, wouldn't you know it, their loved one died before they returned. And every single survivor felt guilty and horrible and like they let their person down.

And then we talk to the departed loved one and they reveal that they waited to die until everyone left because they couldn't bear the bedside drama and agony and crying and they didn't want their loved ones' last memories of them to be in the throes of death. Not only isn't the departed loved one disappointed at all; they chose to die without having their family and friends at their bedside when they crossed over.

So, if you are reading this and you have never had a medium reading and you feel guilty over not being at your loved ones' bedsides when they crossed over, please realize that your departed loved ones do not need to forgive you because you didn't do anything wrong. Their souls determined when it was time for them to cross over and engineered an event that would make that happen.

We're going to talk more about the timing of death in the next chapter when we talk about the circle of life and some more fundamentals related to birth, living and dying. But, while we are on the subject, and as a prelude to the next chapter, I'd like to talk about one more aspect about the fear of dying – because so many people I know worry about the how and the where.

One of the things that I find really interesting as I get older and see that many more of my friends and family members are dealing with serious health issues, is when some of them express this fear of dying during surgery. As a medium, whenever anyone tells me that they are afraid of dying, I usually ask their permission to get right down to the basics and talk about why they shouldn't be afraid. But, I always find it interesting when people say to me that they absolutely are terrified of dying on an operating table.

Hopefully I'm not sounding flippant here, but I have to tell you that dying on an operating table is one of my top three preferred ways to go. I'm not kidding. Just think about it. I would be drugged out of my mind, so feeling no pain and having no physical awareness of any sensation in my body.

I would be surrounded by a team of medical professionals in an environment that is totally equipped to take care of my body afterwards. And, I wouldn't be in the precarious position of having a friend or family member find my dead body and needing to deal with the trauma of finding me, and then dealing with having my body transported elsewhere.

One of my friends tragically lost her niece to a heroin overdose a few years ago, and I went with her when they removed her niece's body from her apartment. And, let me tell you, the memory of that event is still unsettling to me, and I would never wish that experience on anyone.

Seeing your loved one in a body bag being carried out of his or her home is one of those images that is really difficult to forget and it is really, really sad. But, remember, dying at home when no one else is there doesn't mean that the departed person felt abandoned or alone, because we all have a spirit team to protect and assist us during the process.

Let's get back to the operating room scenario. Probably if I was having major surgery, then some of my loved ones would be gathered in the waiting room and they would all be together to support each other if I died. And, they wouldn't have to endure the challenge of being at my bedside and remembering seeing me take my last breath. I could only hope that if I don't die peacefully in my sleep that I am lucky enough to die on an operating table.

I think that dying instantly is also a bonus for the person who crosses over. You can be out there living your life and then BAM – out of nowhere you die instantly from a heart attack, a blood clot in your brain, a massive stroke, or an intense physical trauma that is so devastating that you never knew what hit you. If I can't die on an operating table, or peacefully in my sleep, than dying instantly without ever knowing what hit me is also high up on my list.

I'm really not being sarcastic here. Well, maybe a little irreverent. But, when we die suddenly, it is so much easier for us than suffering through a long, drawn out illness in which we experience overwhelming physical pain, weakness, inability to function physically and/or mentally, and require extensive care.

The down side of dying suddenly is that it is devastating for loved ones who survive because it is shocking and unexpected and nearly impossible for them to wrap their brains around. Also, survivors of those who die suddenly often carry an added, and in my experience, unnecessary burden of guilt. In the second half of the book, we will share some ways for survivors to release guilt and move on from a place of peace.

So, now that we've dispelled some of the myths about what actually happens when humans die, it might be a good time to share some stories about the circle of life –

the timing of birth and death and what souls encounter
and experience when they reach the other side.

Chapter 5

The Circle of Life

*"Energy can neither be created nor destroyed.
It simply changes form."*

-Albert Einstein

When a soul arrives at the other side, it still retains its energetic essence and it's personality from its lifetime on earth. The soul hasn't ceased to exist; it has simply changed form and is back in its original bubble; that encapsulated mass of life force energy we described earlier.

My experience as a medium has taught me that the places we think about as heaven and hell don't exactly exist as actual locations. Every soul arrives at the same destination after crossing over to the other side. That place is where vital force energy gathers, and where groups of souls reside. The location for each specific soul is determined by where its soul group lives.

Soul groups are made up of ancestors, spirit guides and other souls who collaborate with each other to support the evolution of each soul in the group. We'll talk more about soul groups in the next chapter, but for now, just know that our ancestors meet us when we cross over and that our ancestors are members of our soul group.

After moving through the tunnel of light, the soul is welcomed to the other side by members of his or her soul group, including departed pets. Isn't it a comfort to know that your fur babies will be there to greet you? It brings me great comfort, I tell you. And, every soul goes through an assimilation process. The process is the same for everyone, but the actual events differ based on how the person died, and what he or she experienced during the most recent past life.

When a soul integrates into the environment on the other side, then one or more wise members of the soul group are assigned to provide support and guidance. Souls who died traumatically or who experienced severe tragedies in life will be accompanied by a few extra spirit guides for a longer amount of time during this process.

As soon as the soul is able to acknowledge that it has been transported to the other side and is now, in human terms, dead, then it is prepared for the Life Review process. During the Life Review, the soul is introduced to the Akashic Records, where every second of every incarnation is kept. It is kind of like watching a movie of your entire life on Earth, and the purpose is for the soul to experience how every behavior and decision affected others.

When we were generous, and loving and positive and interacted with others from that perspective, we will feel the joy that they experienced. But, when we were fearful, violent, dishonest, or mean, we will also experience how our actions made other people feel. This is the dark part of the Life Review and supported by seasoned members of our soul groups. During the review process, we will assess our actions and the impacts of choices we made during our lives, and this will determine the next steps of our soul journeys.

All of us will experience a Life Review when our souls return to the other side. I have spoken with several of my departed friends and family members about the Life Review process and they all describe it in the same way. Recently, I was lucky to talk with a living person who had a near-death experience and returned. He is the only person I've ever met who came back to his body after completing his Life Review.

Time on the other side moves much faster than time on Earth, so it isn't inconceivable (although I think it is extremely rare) that a soul can cross over, complete a Life Review in a matter of minutes in Earth time and then return to the physical body and continue living. But, I believed this man because he spoke with such complete conviction and said that he still remembers every moment of his current life – every second, every sensation, every emotion and every event – right up until that moment when his soul returned to his body. I think he expected me to be surprised, but I told him that I am a medium and what he described is consistent with what I've been told about the Life Review while communicating with the departed.

When a person dies and the soul decides to remain on the other side, after the Life Review is completed, the soul and its spirit guides determine the level of enlightenment that the soul has reached as a result of action or inaction during the previous lifetime. And then, most soul choose an assignment on the other side, work that they will do until it is time to reincarnate so they can gain maturity and wisdom. Or, maybe the soul realizes that it doesn't require any more incarnations and decides to become a spirit guide. Spirit guides have different assignments, but typically work to support and teach individuals on Earth or groups of souls on the other side.

I believe that souls actually choose to incarnate into a living vessel for one of two reasons – to learn lessons and evolve spiritually, and/or to make a contribution by fulfilling a life purpose and influencing the soul journeys of others. I also believe that the lessons and purpose are determined before the soul incarnates.

This concept of pre-determined soul lessons and purpose has been validated for me by studying astrology. I think that souls choose their dates, places and times of birth, their parents and families of origin, their gender, nationality, and physical appearance to influence their soul journeys.

We can learn about these choices by analyzing the natal astrological chart, through Akashic Record readings, and also through past-life regression hypnosis. I recently met someone in Santa Fe who actually does past life regression astrology as well.

While astrology is an ancient art and science, other methods of accessing information about past lives are relatively recent modalities that are becoming increasingly popular as healing therapies. They are effective at helping to heal from past and present life trauma and can assist us in getting unstuck, resolving persistent challenges, and progressing on our journeys.

Earlier we spoke about souls having assignments on the other side. Some souls actually work for the greater good. One of my friends who had been an environmental engineer passed away at the young age of 53. He died suddenly, from a heart attack and was unable to be revived. He was the first person I knew who went to the other side after I had developed my Mediumship abilities. And, he showed up at my house suddenly a few days after he crossed over.

All mediums receive messages from spirit in different ways. I'm primarily clairvoyant, and that means that I actually see the departed person's image, usually of their face or their upper body in a bubble. Usually the bubble is floating in the upper left hand corner of whatever wall is in front of me.

I have really good boundaries with spirits and rarely receive messages from spirits I don't know or from unwelcome spirits. But when friends and family members cross over, or if I really click with a particular spirit during a medium reading, from time to time that spirit will show up and initiate communications with me.

The first time a departed friend or family member connects with me is usually within a few days after they cross over. They know that I am a medium and they also know that I will be able to see them and converse with them. It sounds kind of weird and creepy, but actually it isn't scary at all.

Every time it occurs, it validates to me that the departed one is alive and happy in spirit. And, even though the person typically just appears; it is interesting that I never feel as though a boundary has been violated because it a person I know and adore. They usually show up in broad daylight when I'm at my desk in my home office and dressed, thank goodness!

My friend Michael was the first spirit who popped in to see me a few days after he crossed over. We had a very interesting conversation. In the beginning, and this is also typical of recently departed souls, they are still becoming accustomed to not being constrained by a body and so they float, and fly, and sometimes even do flips. They are usually excited and joyful and amazed.

Michael started teasing me, showing himself sitting with his legs crossed and levitating. He also provided some messages for his wife, who was also my friend, about songs that were special to them, trips they had taken, and validation that he was having lots of fun on the other side.

This is another thing that happens that is so interesting to me. Even though the departed realize that their passing caused pain and suffering to those they left behind; they don't typically express any regrets about being on the other side. They are usually overjoyed to be in a state of bliss and to be free from their bodies. Strange, I know.

Michael also shared with me that he had crossed over when he did because his skills were needed. He is the first spirit to share with me that souls are actually being called to the other side to assist with repairing some of the issues that we humans have created that are destructive to a peaceful, healthy environment on Earth. Michael had been passionate about water conservation when he was alive, and he explained to me that our water situation was even more precarious than he had realized, even though he knew it was bad.

His job on the other side is to work with other souls who have knowledge about water to try to influence positive progress in water conservation and pollution. He explained that no matter how much his family missed him; that his responsibilities on the other side were much more important and his knowledge was needed for the greater good and that he died when it was time for him to do so.

Michael isn't the first person I've known who felt that they crossed over when the time was right. Sometimes, people know that they are going to die before it happens, even when the cause of their passing is from a sudden accident. Often these individuals are highly evolved souls, intimately in touch with spiritual energy.

And Sean Stephenson was one of those people. I've never met a person like him. Sean was a purveyor of love and joy, a phenomenal teacher, and a truly unique human being.

If you've never heard of him, you can learn more about his story by visiting his Facebook page[5] (it has nearly a million followers) reading one of his books, viewing his Tedx talk[6], or watching the documentary about his life entitled "3 Foot Giant." Sean's life was a testament to identifying one's purpose and demonstrating how to fulfill that mission magnificently.

Born with the condition osteogenesis imperfecta (also known as brittle bone disease), Sean wasn't expected to live for one day on this Earth. He actually survived for forty incredible years. Sean's mobility was dependent upon a wheelchair, and he was only three feet tall.

During his lifetime, Sean shared inspiring speeches with millions of people and reached millions more through videos on social media and YouTube. His message was that he was put on the planet to help people overcome their insecurities. Most people are impressed by the fact that Sean worked in the Clinton White House, was a friend of Tony Robbins, rubbed elbows with Sir Richard Branson, and even appeared on the Oprah show.

But, I am in awe of Sean's insight, his alignment with spirit, his dedication to service evidenced by his PhD in clinical hypnotherapy, his production of training materials and workshops teaching others how to share their stories with the world through public speaking, and his infectious, incredible, positive attitude and sense of humor.

I met Sean when I attended one of his 10K speeches workshops in Scottsdale, Arizona. It was kind of crazy because I decided to attend two days before it started. I learned about Sean from a coaching guru I was following, and felt a strong calling to attend the training. Sean on video is captivating. Meeting Sean in person was like being in the presence of Yoda.

Before I met Sean, I'd been fortunate to meet and work with many people facing seemingly daunting medical challenges. When I was in my twenties, I volunteered at Children's Hospital of Denver in the Rehabilitation and Oncology ward for three years. I worked with kids with cancer and spent hours talking with their parents and siblings.

I also spent time every week hanging out with kids with physically challenging conditions such as spina bifida, full or partial paralysis after injuries, cystic fibrosis and muscular dystrophy. All of those kids were limited in their mobility and vitality, but each of them was special, and the lessons I learned from them were priceless.

But meeting Sean Stephenson took things to an entirely different level. Deciding at an early age to view his physical situation as a gift rather than a burden, Sean radiated stability, optimism and wisdom. And even though I wasn't able to attend more of his workshops, the things I learned from him and from the incredible humans who were other students of Sean's, will stay with me forever.

Most people who have met Sean remember him for telling them he loved them. But, Sean didn't say that to me. Sean told me "I see you." And it is very interesting because even though I have people who love me, I've always felt misunderstood and like people don't really get who I am. But, it gives me great comfort to know that Sean connected with what I needed most and told me that he could see and appreciate who I am.

For a few years before his passing, Sean experienced one life threatening accident each year and navigated the tightrope between life and death. Each time, he was able to tough it out and remain on this side, but last summer, on August 28, 2019, Sean's wheelchair tipped over and he sustained a life-threatening brain injury.

In her touching speech at Sean's Celebration of Life, his wife, Mindie Kniss shared the fact that she believed that Sean knew he was going to cross over. She explained that two days before his passing, he did something unusual; he cancelled plans to go swimming with his friends and decided to stay home and spend time with her. She also explained that Sean made several phone calls that week to make amends with people. She also shared Sean's final words.

Sean was the master of delivering life-changing wisdom in a few sentences. And, in alignment with him being his ever wise and amazing self, moments before he was wheeled into surgery, Sean told Mindie and his friends who were at his bedside. "This isn't happening TO me. This is happening FOR me."

Sean lived true to his purpose even in his final hours on Earth. His last words were profound, prophetic, and in alignment with his mission. And for all of us who remain and grieve for him, those last elegant sentences he shared enable us to release any insecurity we might have had about his passing. And his words indicate that his death was going to be positive and beneficial for him, and confirm what we've determined so far. Death is a natural part of life.

Fortunately, Sean crossed over on the operating table. And for that, I am grateful because as we talked about earlier – it really is one of the best ways to go. Like so many other things he did in his life, Sean got his finale right. Way to go, Sean!

I only met Sean once, even though I interacted with him several times. And, I never knew until I saw the video of his Celebration of Life that his best friends called him Seanie. Like most of the other departed people I knew when they were alive, Sean showed up in the corner of my room a few days after he crossed over. I was kind of surprised that he would reach out to me, but Sean knew that I was a medium and departed spirits seem to get excited when they are able communicate directly with a medium when they are settling in on the other side.

Of course, Sean was hilarious, and true to his personality, when he appeared to me, it was comical. Sean was seated cross-legged in meditation pose with his palms turned upward on his knees and his thumbs touching his index fingers (Sean always rocked the little details). He was levitating up and down as if sitting on a cloud. When I acknowledged his presence, he then began to morph into different life-sized super heroes, complete with costumes, and began showing me that he was overjoyed with being tall and powerful and muscular, and most of all - able to fly without being encumbered by his human body.

He started out as Mighty Mouse, and then expanded to a full-sized Spiderman, Batman (this one was all about the eyes), and finally Superman. Sean loved the comedic value of dressing up in costumes when he was on the planet, and is thrilled that he has a complete wardrobe and props department at his disposal on the other side. He joked that he is now a fashionista! He even did this Ninja move where he ran up the walls and across the ceiling and back down again. I just sat there and laughed with him.

He didn't give me specific messages to share with people, but I did discover that Seanie was his special name. I feel like Sean didn't have any more messages because he had already shared them with those who were near and dear to him – right up until the moment of his passing. Unlike most of us, Sean realized that his life could end at any moment and so he lived with gusto and communicated succinctly, honestly and directly. Living life to its fullest and making every moment count were a few of his many gifts.

But, when he was bouncing around my bedroom, he did joke with me and told me that he had arrived alive ;-) And, he also shared that he was having a complete and total blast on the other side being able to transform into any body he desired and experience the thrill of unrestricted movement. He also told me that he would assist me in fulfilling my mission of helping others creating new paradigms for moving forward after loss, and that he would continue to send new clients and supportive people to me.

Many of us try to make a difference, but the fact that Sean was on the planet, truly made the world a better place. When I think about Sean rocking on from the other side, I hear the words of the guru Rafiki from Lion King in my head, explaining to Simba that his departed father Mufasa lives on in him. And, I believe that Sean Stephenson lives on within every person he touched during his incredible journey. His legacy is exceptionally infinite.

Hopefully these stories have provided some insight about the timing of death, the fact that the soul lives on, and that Mediumship is a very real phenomenon. And now that we've explored what happens when someone dies, and what we will likely encounter when we reach the other side; I'd like to start exploring how departed loved ones are connected to the living, some of the thoughts they share from the other side, and what their hopes tend to be for those who remain behind.

Chapter 6

Resting in Power – Living in Peace

"Look at the stars. The great kings of the past look down on us from those stars. So, whenever you feel alone, just remember that those kings will be there to guide you. And, so will I."

- Mufasa in Disney's "The Lion King"

Resting in power. I discovered this message today on Facebook from a post written by a guy named Winston Ben Clement, and it really resonated with me. Because after working as a professional medium for ten years, every single soul with whom I've communicated is resting in power! They are in a place of peace, but are so overjoyed to be living outside of the restrictions that being human imposes. We're going to talk about this concept in this chapter to help lift the burden of grief.

Earlier, we mentioned the timing of death, and that a person's soul always decides when it is time to cross over. This concept is a little bit tricky to wrap one's mind around because most of us have been taught that when someone dies, it is usually somebody's fault. In my experience, this isn't true at all.

As mediums, many of us attract similar types of clients, depending on what is happening in our lives at the time. For many years, especially when I first began working as a medium, people who had lost spouses at a young age booked sessions with me. Sometimes the person had died in a tragic accident, left home one morning and never came back again. Other times, the person died at a young age from a terminal illness.

One of the typical outcomes of these types of situations is that the survivors feel very guilty about their loved one's passing – and usually about events that happened before, during or after the person died. And, what is also consistent is that the departed loved ones don't have any animosity about any of those things. In reality, the guilt isn't necessary.

Now I'd like to share a story that addresses the cause and timing of death from an actual medium reading I did many years ago, and I still remember most of the details because the lessons were so profound. I share this with my client's permission.

This was one of those situations in which a young wife felt guilty for her husband's death, and even believed that had she acted differently, he would still be alive. She carried a tremendous burden and felt that she could have and should have prevented his death. As we know from previous chapters, the soul decides when to cross over. This story will help explain why.

My client was a woman named Michelle. Michelle was thirty three years old and had a three year old son. Her husband, Jack was a few years older than she was. Jack was diabetic and they both worked together to monitor his condition.

One evening, Jack told Michelle that he didn't feel well. He suspected that he was getting the flu. Since it was Sunday night, and Jack wasn't feeling really badly, they decided to not go to the ER and not to call the doctor. The next morning, Jack stayed home, and Michelle took their son to daycare and went to work.

Later that afternoon, Michelle and her son returned home to find Jack's body on the living room floor. He had died earlier that day. Michelle's instant reaction was that she had caused her husband's death. She should have taken him to the ER on Sunday night. She should have insisted that he go to the doctor. Michelle's sister was referred to me by a friend of mine who was a metaphysical practitioner, but not a medium. Michelle's sister wisely insisted that Michelle schedule a session with me.

Jack, as it turned out, was one of those talkative people and he was a bit of a jokester, and really funny. Within just a few minutes of connecting with him, he starting sharing messages with me. First of all, he wanted Michelle to know that he was doing great and that he was fine. He also shared some messages about their son and indicated that he shows up in his bedroom when he is sleeping and that the dog always knows he is there.

He then started sharing funny anecdotes with me so that Michelle was sure we were indeed talking with Jack. He was one of those souls that mediums live to read for. He mentioned jokes that they had shared and information about their son and how much they had loved their lives together. Finally, he shared information about the day he died.

Jack explained that what happened was that he didn't realize at the time, but the symptoms he was experiencing were related to his diabetes. On the day he died, he actually slipped into a diabetic coma. The whole thing came out of nowhere, and he didn't realize it before. But, he also explained that he crossed over at the appropriate time and that he had work to do on the other side that called his soul back there.

And, then he told Michelle that it was so perfect that he died the way he did. At this point, I was in complete shock, but I shared the message.

Jack went on to explain that he would have gone into the coma with or without medical intervention. And, if he would have gone into the coma at a hospital, then they would have put him on life support. Michelle would have had to make the decision to pull the plug. Also, Jack's family was very conservative and he was convinced that they would have fought her every step of the way.

Michelle and Jack had talked about what would happen if he ever went into a coma, and he told her in no uncertain terms that he would want to die naturally. So, the fact that he died when he did avoided many burdens for Michelle. She didn't have to pay huge medical expenses associated with being in a coma in a hospital. She didn't have to make the decision herself to take Jack off of life support. She didn't have to deal with his family and all of the drama that would have ensued.

We were also able to talk about what happened when Jack crossed over. He wanted to be very clear and make sure that I told Michelle these very words, "I didn't suffer at all. I didn't die alone. I wasn't scared. It was actually awesome." Then Jack went on to explain the tunnel of light, being surrounded by love and helpful spirits, and being greeted on the other side by family members and pets. He essentially told the same story as Kate had shared with me when she said that "dying is the easiest thing I ever did in my life."

Fortunately, Michelle was able to experience the healing power of Mediumship firsthand. Jack delivered the messages she needed to forgive herself and move forward. He also was the first departed person to thank me for the work I am doing, and every time that has happened since then, tears well up in my eyes.

Jack also shared with Michelle that his wishes for her and their son was that they know he loves them and is with them; that they live happily ever after; that they part with his possessions as they feel comfortable; that they move to a different house if that is less painful; and that they find peace knowing that everything happened according to a Divine plan.

Jack was also a highly evolved soul. And the messages he shared are consistent with what I hear during almost every medium reading in which a survivor is grieving after losing a loved one. It's kind of confusing to understand how someone we loved deeply can transition to the other side and not feel sad that they left us. I think it is because the other side is pure, loving light. It is ultimate peace. It is paradise.

Also, as the departed continue to assimilate there, they gradually become disconnected from the day-to-day memories and their identities as human beings on Earth. Within about five years, they actually begin to forget their human names. They also receive wisdom from their journey there, and realize that the things they thought were important as humans; are mostly insignificant in the greater scheme of the vast possibilities of the Universe.

Another thing I've experienced over and over again during medium readings is that the departed don't carry regret, anger or animosity toward the living. If you had a fight with your person the morning they died; it really doesn't matter to the departed. If his brother did something really stupid at the memorial service and you are still feeling mortified, rest assured that your departed loved one isn't upset about it, and even though most departed souls are present in spirit at their own funerals, memorial services, and celebrations of life, they don't judge what happened or didn't happen.

The most important things for you to know if you are grieving the loss of a loved one are: 1) Let go of the guilt. 2) Your person is with you in spirit and sends you messages in the form of feathers, coins, animals or insects, the disruption of lights and electrical devices, playing songs on the radio, and by sending messages about a shared love you had – flowers, a movie or fictional character, etc. Your DLO also often speaks to you through your dreams. 3) Your mission, should you decide to accept it is to get your feet back under you and move on with your life. They not only give you permission, but their greatest desire is for you to be happy and healthy and loved.

I'm feeling as though I need to emphasize that last sentence one more time. Your departed loved one, even if that person was your life partner, your spouse, your fiancé, or your soul mate – wants you to live and love again. It doesn't matter whether that person was your child, your best friend, or your sibling, they want you to experience joy and laughter and love. Because their primary desire for you is for you to be happy. They are resting in power and they want you to live in peace.

Even though I've been so fortunate to train and get to know some of the world's top mediums, I must admit that I have a special respect for John Holland. I've seen him working live on stage many times. And to me, he is the consummate medium because of his unwavering dedication to serving spirit and survivors, and because of the respectful and tender manner in which he delivers messages.

The first time I saw John on stage, I had just learned that I was a medium and so I analyzed every move he made, every reading he did, and every word he shared. I remember one particular reading that so beautifully illustrates the intention that our departed loved ones have for us. I can share this reading without permission because it happened in a public situation at a live event.

The reading was heartbreaking. The woman for whom John was delivering messages was young. She appeared to be in her late teens or early twenties. As she held the microphone, her hands were shaking. Tears were streaming down her face.

The person she had lost was her fiancé. And it was obvious from her behavior that they shared a deep and soulful love and that her entire life was shattered after losing him. I'm not positive, but I have a feeling that his passing was caused by something instant like a motorcycle accident. John was delivering messages for her, and all of the sudden, out of the blue, I remember John saying. "He is asking you not to get the tattoo."

I still get goose bumps and tears are pouring down my face as I remember this. This woman was planning to get a tattoo of her departed fiancé's name so that she could remember him forever, and feel connected to him every day. She told John this after he delivered her loved one's request.

John then went on to gently explain that she was young and that she had a full life ahead of her. Her departed fiancé wanted her to love other people and to marry someone she adored and to have a beautiful and happy life. She was shocked that he told her to marry someone else. But, that is really the huge lesson in all of this.

Her fiancé crossed over at a very young age because his soul decided it was time for it to go. And even though he wasn't with his true love on Earth, he was thriving on the other side connected with the pure love and joy in that environment and surrounded by the loving energy of his soul group.

What I find especially poignant about this story is that her fiancé was so determined to deliver this message to her that he moved ahead of all of those spirits who were standing in line to have John share their messages. There must have been 300 people in the audience that day.

And, I'm also touched with the fact that John shared this particular, specific, validating and life-changing message with this darling young woman. Mediumship is real, and when done properly, it heals in profound and specific ways.

Now that we've explored what happens on the other side, it is time to offer some information and simple tools you can use to move forward on your healing journey with a new sense of certainty, stability, peacefulness and joy. And, I promise you one thing. It is going to be much easier than you expect it to be.

Chapter 7

Building a New Foundation

*"We could never learn to be brave and patient
if there was only joy in the world."*

- Hellen Keller

Up until this point, I've shared a great deal of knowledge that I obtained during my work as a medium. But now, I'd like to shift direction a bit and start sharing some practical information that I've learned in the twenty-one years since I experienced a life-changing brain injury.

I developed this protocol so that I could get out of bed in the morning and walk across the room. When doctors at the highly acclaimed Craig Rehabilitation Hospital told me I would never work again and that by now I would be in a wheelchair, the 40 year old management consultant that I was then refused to accept the prognosis.

They also told me that I needed to start taking Prozac (a popular anti-depressant at the time) pain killers and sleeping pills or I wouldn't be able to make it through the day. This just didn't make sense to me, and so I never took a pill. We're going to be talking about prescription drugs a bit later, but the good news is that I didn't go there, because if I would have taken their advice, I would now be a wheelchair-bound opioid addict.

Thankfully I was able to use the part of my brain that was still functioning to do the research that led me to explore alternative therapies and also take advantage of my organizational skills to develop a formula for living that would enable me to thrive.

It turns out that losing a loved one and sustaining a life-disabling injury have several things in common. They are traumatic. They are overwhelming. And, after they occur, life as we know it will never be the same. So even though my journey isn't identical to yours, the fundamentals are similar.

I feel that it is just an added bonus that most of the things I learned while healing myself after my own physical trauma are also highly effective in supporting people who are grieving. These processes and techniques have been proven with my clients and now I'm happy to share them with you to support you in navigating you own healing journey.

Now it is time for us to work together so you can begin to build a new and solid foundation that will provide stability as you start to get your life back on track. I promise, there's nothing to fear. What we will share in the final chapters of the book will be painless, and will gradually release the burdens you have been carrying.

One of the first things that happen after we experience a severe trauma or loss is that we learn very quickly who is with us and who can't handle it. After my injury, I found that people in my inner circle either stood up to support me or instantly vanished.

The other thing I realized, and this was especially difficult for me, was that I needed help with some things. I just couldn't manage everything by myself in the beginning. So, it was inevitable that I had to learn to ask others for help. And, you have probably realized this, also.

But, I didn't need people to feel sorry for me or join me in pity parties. I needed people who could do real tasks to help me minimize the stress of existing. So, the first thing I needed to do to build my foundation and solidify my daily infrastructure was to identify who was sincerely available to help me and what was reasonable for me to ask them to do.

So, here are some questions for you to think about as you go through the process of reaching out to others for support.

When you think about your friends and family – who feels the most comforting to you? These are probably the people who don't get all up in your business and don't push emotional buttons. They are the people who don't drive you crazy when you are feeling stressed. And, they are also often people who just roll up their sleeves and help. Think about friends, family members, work colleagues and people from social groups such as school, church, etc.

Before you ask for help outside of your inner circle, it is a good idea to determine what you need most. For me, in the beginning, I just needed to cover the basics – food, housekeeping, and transportation. You may find that that's what you need, also. Then as soon as I was able to survive and get through the day, I felt as though I needed emotional support, someone who could just listen and ask how they could help without being preachy or judging me. And, I personally believe that psychotherapy isn't necessarily your only option here.

After emotional trauma, many of us have physical symptoms or issues. And, if you need pain relief, I encourage you to seek out metaphysical practitioners rather than prescription pain killers (they actually hamper your healing process and we will go into this in a future chapter when we talk about how to get stronger.)

Some great pain relieving and relaxing therapies include massage or chiropractic care (if you prefer physical therapies) or jin shin jyutsu, cranio-sacral massage, or energy healing (there are many types and we will talk all about this in a future chapter). If you have a strong, persistent pain caused by frustration or anger, then I recommend acupuncture.

If you don't know all of the people you need, then ask a master networker. We all know master networkers. They are the people who always know the best florist, the best caterer, the best dentist, and the best hair stylist. They are hub people and they give great referrals. Sometimes people think they are great at this, and they actually are awful. The way to determine if someone is a reliable referral hub is to ask them how they know the person to whom they are referring you.

Also, when you are brainstorming about all of this, write down what you are thinking and don't edit your gut reactions. Also, don't worry about financial cost. Just make a list of your top priorities.

If you've lost a spouse, then you probably need assistance with legal and/or financial decisions or management. If you don't already know people, then you can ask your hub people to give you suggestions.

We are going to approach this subject more in future chapters, but for now, you just need to get the basics covered.

Also, here's one final thing for you to consider. It is acceptable and actually preferable for you to say "no." If your daughter-in-law is well intentioned, but is a control freak that irritates you like nails on a chalkboard, then create some distance from her. If your next door neighbor is a gossiping busy body who just loves to create drama during your misery, then don't answer the door when she drops by. And, it is also ok to take a break from phone calls and social media contacts whenever interacting with those people just drives you nuts. Now is the time for you to seek support, simplify and find solace.

After you finish brainstorming, identify the three most important things with which you need help now. Write the names of the people whom you need to contact, and reach out to them this week and ask for assistance. If this feels overwhelming, then ask a close friend or family member to help.

As soon as you have your basic infrastructure under control, it is a good time to clear out the stale, depressing energy that is lingering in your body, and also probably in your home. Now we are going to get a little bit woo woo, but that is where the magic is. Because going to the root cause of your pain and suffering – the energy – is where you will clear out the cobwebs and create momentum for healing.

One of the most significant things I've learned during my own healing journey – and it is interesting that I just became aware of it a few years ago – is the concept of energy in the body impacting wellness. When I trained as a healer using Spring Forest Qi Gong, my teacher (a qi gong master) explained that all disease is caused by energetic blockages. When energy moves freely through the body, then the body heals itself.

One of the premier scientists doing research about cellular energy and how it affects wellness is Dr. Bruce Lipton. According to Dr. Lipton, the body both absorbs and radiates energetic vibration. Good vibes heal. Bad vibes cause disease.[7] If you want to learn more, then click on the end-note link and read his fascinating article about "The Wisdom of Your Cells."

As I worked as a medium and healer helping trauma survivors to move forward, it also occurred to me that the memory of both physical and emotional trauma remains within our cellular systems until it is cleared. And, because these vibes are by definition, negative, I believe that they initially cause pain and suffering and that throbbing sensation we feel energetically after loss. And, over time, if left untreated, I believe that the cellular memory of the trauma can cause disease. This has been confirmed by scientific research.[8]

What I discovered when I first began recommending organic healing (an energy healing modality I developed combining Spring Forest Qi Gong and my own clairvoyant and clairsentient abilities) to my medium clients who were grieving, we discovered that after a single session, they felt lighter and some described that for the first time, they didn't feel intense physical and emotional pain. Some told me that the burden they had been carrying since their loved one died had been lifted. Others felt more energized and positive and had more energy to rebuild their lives.

After appearing on one of my favorite podcasts called the Insightful Astrology podcast, hosted by the brilliant New York-based astrologer, Maria DeSimone, a new client came to me for a session. She was in her early thirties and signed up for energy healing after hearing me talk about the benefits on the podcast. The woman, Danielle had lost her mother at a young age and was still recovering from the loss. She also had a sister who was two years older and she referred her sister to me.

These darling sisters became two of my most favorite clients. They both scheduled energy clearing and then decided to schedule a Mediumship session that the two of them attended together. Normally I don't conduct sessions with more than one client, but I made an exception in this case because I knew that they wouldn't talk over each other and that it would probably be more effective for them to experience the session together. I'm sharing this story with their permission.

We were able to connect with their darling mother, and even though she was one of those quiet types who usually preferred being behind the scenes, she showed up like a champ and shared specific information that validated to her daughters that their mother was alive and well in spirit.

The goal of Mediumship from my perspective is to always share one specific message that resonates so strongly with my client that they know for sure it came from their departed loved one. And, we were able to do this several times during the reading. The sisters were in their early teens when their mother crossed over and the loss had affected both of their lives.

After the session, they both sent me separate emails to let me know how much they appreciated the session. They also described in their own individual ways that the grief burden they had been carrying for over twenty years was gone. They were no longer suffering. They felt relieved, optimistic and thankful.

This is one of so many stories about how the combination of energy healing and Mediumship create a new foundation from which to move forward on the healing journey. They are both important, but energy healing is fundamental.

While traumatic memory resides in our cellular systems; I've also discovered that it gathers within the chakra systems, the energy centers described in ayuervedic medicine as influencing body, mind, and spirit.

As part of my organic healing regimen, I also clear, heal and balance the chakra system. Understanding the chakra system can also help us to open up areas in which we feel stuck in our lives. So, if you are having a life issue, it is probably influenced by one or more chakras. And, clearing and balancing can release whatever is holding you back.

For example, the first chakra is the root chakra. It influences physical and financial safety and security. So, if you never are able to settle down in a permanent location and if your life lacks stability and financial security, balancing this chakra might help.

Here is some brief information about the chakras. I explain them like parts of a car. We could teach a five day class on chakras, but I think it is beneficial to have a basic understanding. Also, chakras can be damaged from both present and past life trauma. I provide services to heal present life damage with organic healing. I also offer something called a Soul Harmony session that has proven effective for spiritually evolved people who are willing to get out of the box in terms of their energetic growth.

Each chakra has a color and chakras balance from the bottom up. Here's some more information about the chakra systems and how healing damage or blockages can positively impact your life:

- Chakra 1 – Root – Red – Like the wheels on a car. Your connection with the earth. Facilitates safety and security, financial stability and the ability to find and settle in a permanent home.

- Chakra 2 – Pelvic – Orange – Gas tank – where you get your fuel, motivation, passion, and creativity. Facilitates evolution and transformation, getting unstuck, feeling more energized, and generating excitement in life.

- Chakra 3 – Solar Plexus – Yellow – Engine – your energy center. Your core. Facilitates balance and knowing, career stability, finding and keeping your dream job, and feeling peaceful and confident.

- Chakra 4 – Heart – Green (color of love and money) – Steering wheel – where you chart your course. "Lead with your heart." Facilitates forgiveness, healing, joy, expressing love, and finding your soul partner.

- Chakra 5 – Throat – Light blue – Body and style – How you communicate. Facilitates empowerment and self-expression, the ability to communicate assertively and to speak up for yourself when you need to instead of keeping quiet.

- Chakra 6 – Third Eye – Indigo Blue – Windshield – How you see clearly. Facilitates wisdom, knowing, and heightened perception that helps you to view your life clearly, as well as facilitating intuition, especially clairvoyant abilities.

- Chakra 7 – Crown Chakra – Violet/White – Radio – Your connection to a higher power, the Universe and cosmic energy. Facilitates enlightenment and receiving energy and information from the Creator, Ascended Masters, the angelic realm and spirit guides.

Clearing, healing and balancing your energy removes the debilitating energetic memory of traumatic events. Several types of energetic therapy can assist with this process including jin shin jyutsu (I love this therapy because it is energy healing that uses meridians similar to acupuncture) and cranio-sacral massage. Some metaphysical practitioners like me have created our own methodologies for this type of healing.

To take your healing to the next level and diminish feelings of depression, pain, suffering and hopelessness, you can consider scheduling an energy clearing session with an energy healer. The Lightwalker Beacon Network has some amazing ones and we all work over the phone, so you can choose a healer in any location. You can access our online resource center at lightwalkerlife.com.

Another important thing to consider when moving forward on a healing journey is to focus on what you have and what you have learned and gained from the experience instead of dwelling on what you lost.

One of the things that I've learned in my life journey when it seemed as though I was on a roller coaster ride with career direction, financial stability, gaining and losing dream homes, obtaining and losing material possessions, gaining and losing control over my life and physical wellness, and experiencing tragic deaths of family and friends – is that nothing is permanent. Nothing.

At one point in my life, I was fortunate to train as a hospice volunteer, although I moved out of the area before I was able to serve. We did this exercise that really resonated with me. Our instructor asked us to write down the top 5 things in our lives that we valued. And, then she asked us to cross out one of the things to symbolize losing that thing. Eventually, she asked us to cross off every single one of those things. She then explained that how we now felt was how people in hospice feel. They face losing everything they valued in their lives on Earth, one thing at a time.

But, at some point, all of us will face releasing the ability of having specific careers, spouses, homes, possessions, friends, pets, family members, and even finances. I'm not trying to sound gloomy here, but in reality, wouldn't it be better to just acknowledge that none of these things really defines who we are or how valuable our lives are? Wouldn't it be easier to take each day and each experience as it comes and to be grateful for what we have and treasure and cherish today?

People who learn to detach end up being happier. According to Family Living magazine, here is a list of habits of happy people:[9]

Live in the moment. Whenever I work with people who are overwhelmed with stress after trauma, one of the first things I recommend is that they focus on what they need to achieve in smaller increments. Don't worry about tomorrow or next week or next month or next year or the next five years. Depending on how daunting your day seems, focus on what you need to do this morning or this afternoon or even in the next hour.

Be generous. There's a reason why the old adage, it is better to give than to receive has stood the test of time. One of the things that really helped me in my twenties when I had experienced a really stupid marriage to a pathological liar and divorced within a few months; was to work as a volunteer. Back then, I was an over-achiever, so chose to volunteer at Children's Hospital of Denver in rehabilitation and oncology.

I worked there one evening a week for about three years, and every night when I went home I was so grateful for my healthy body, and the freedom to do what I wanted without having to worry about having a child with cancer or challenged with health and mobility.

Spend time outdoors in sunlight. I actually think that spending time outdoors in nature is just as good and even when it is snowing or raining, breathing fresh air and moving is soothing to mind, body, and spirit. Whenever you feel down, taking a walk can really help lift your spirits.

Acknowledge negative feelings. I agree that suppressing grief or sadness is toxic. Sometimes as an energy healer, I work with clients who carry stress in their shoulders or shove it down into their stomachs. But, I've also learned that right after expressing a negative emotion, it is a good idea to think of a solution or a remedy. When we think about Universal law, what we focus on repeats. So, when we affirm how sad and depressed we feel, we are really telling the Universe to keep on sending sadness and depression because that is our reality.

But if we use affirmations like "I'm still sad, but I'm feeling more positive every day and am choosing to continue to live my life with optimism," then that creates hope and possibilities. I'm not an advocate of seeking out groups that provide a "safe place to suffer." To me, there is no such thing as a safe place to suffer because suffering creates negative vibes and as we talked about earlier, negative vibes create disease.

Value time over money. When I think about all of the people I know, the people with the most money tend to have the least amount of time. And the people with the least money tend to have more time. That isn't completely true, because some people work two and three jobs just to make ends meet. But, when someone shares their time, it feels more valuable to me than when they share their money. Money comes and goes, but investing time in something builds.

Smile more often. I love this one. The protocol I developed to recover from my own physical trauma cites six things that release stress for everyone. They include laughter, de-cluttering our physical environments, spending time in nature, spending time with animals, meditation and prayer, and getting a medium reading. If you want to feel happier instantly, find something to laugh about.

This chapter has given us quite a few things to think about when it comes to building a new foundation. You don't need to do all of them, but just pick and choose the ones that really speak to you.

Before we move on to the next chapter where we will explore how we view our current life realities, I just want to add one more piece of information. This is the thing that saved me in the very beginning after my brain injury, when I felt like my whole world was shattered. And, that thing was creating some new routines to provide predictability and make managing my day easier.

I'm a morning person, and one of the things that helps me thrive and do all of the things I do better – is to have a morning routine. I find that when I can stick to my routine that everything just works. Here is a list of things you can potentially start doing each morning to set you up for a more peaceful day.

Drink a satisfying beverage. I actually find that starting my day with these beverages really helps me start with a calm perspective. You can experiment with beverages that make you feel better. For me, I start my day with a 1 oz shot of a liquid herbal supplement called Ionix Supreme from a company called Isagenix. (If you are interested in getting some, let me know and I can get you a discount).

This herbal infusion contains adaptogens (herbs that relieve stress). When I first started using this product, I was working on improving health and wellness. One day I ran out of it and had to wait three days for my next order to ship. Wow, did I feel the difference. Needless to say, I'll never be without it again.

I'm also a coffee person. There's a lot of information out there about the benefits and detriments of drinking coffee. But for me, coffee just makes me happy. Here are some things to keep in mind about coffee. Organic is best – adding pesticides to boiling water helps us ingest them faster. Low-acid dark roasts are best because they help our bodies to be alkaline.

Also, I think one and at the most, two cups a day is the limit. Coffee can disrupt the digestive tract when high qualities are ingested and it can also create a dependence on caffeine or make people jittery. I drink black coffee and would never, ever add sugar. Finally, drink coffee in a glass mug and avoid Styrofoam cups. You can also drink it from an aluminum container.

Trader Joe's has a great selection of these coffees. When I want an extra-special treat, I use organic, herbal-infused coffee from Wildcrafter Botanicals created by the wise sage Tieraona Low Dog, MD who is also a master herbalist and lives east of Santa Fe, New Mexico (so she is practically my neighbor). You can check out her amazing coffee at wildcrafter.com. My favorite is the Creative Genius blend that assists with focus. But they also have other blends that boost energy, help strengthen the immune system, and make you feel calm.

I also love tea as a breakfast beverage, especially in the winter. If you drink tea, you can become a total connoisseur and explore thousands of types and options. When I drink tea, I stick with Organic. In the morning, I opt for a caffeinated tea and in the afternoon, go strictly for herbal. I've also found that drinking peppermint tea before bed really helps me sleep soundly and doesn't give me nightmares as chamomile or sleep blends tend to do.

Make your bed. If you've never seen the video of the 2014 University of Texas commencement address delivered by the former Navy Seal trainer, Admiral William H. McRaven about the value of making your bed, I recommend you click on this endnote and check it out.[10] It takes about twenty minutes but I find it to be highly motivational. Making your bed first thing in the morning starts your day by completing a successful task and also makes things feel ordered. Making your bed can also help you sleep better because your bed linens will be smooth, even and uniform.

Stretch. According to yoga master Rodney Yee, "In the morning the body is rested, but stiff from inactivity." I love his yoga DVD called AM/PM yoga, available at Amazon or gaiam.com. According to Rodney, this gentle yoga series "awakens the body and mind." It takes about twenty minutes to do, but really helps start the day with a sense of calmness and fresh energy. I like exercising at home because I have a space in which to do it and no people here to distract me. It also saves time because I don't have to drive before or after. You can find a DVD that you like, or simply do some simple stretches to help you start your day.

Eat a nutritious breakfast. Grandma always said that breakfast is the most important meal of the day, and I happen to agree. I used to eat protein for breakfast and for me that was meat and potatoes or oatmeal with butter, honey and almond milk. Both of these breakfasts gave me the stable energy I needed to do my work as a healer and medium. Now, I'm addicted to the Isagenix plant-based vanilla chai protein powder and greens mix. I have a protein shake using these ingredients almost every morning and this one simple routine has changed my energy and my physical strength.

Again, with breakfast foods, I like to avoid overly processed food, sugar, chemicals and pesticides. So meat is organic and/or free range and/or doesn't contain chemicals. Cereal or grains are also organic and avoid white flour and white sugar. I also monitor my fruit intake, although I do love bananas because some fruits are high in sugar. Blueberries and raspberries are lower in sugar and also help minimize inflammation in the body.

Discover breakfast foods that energize you and keep a good supply in your home. Enjoying a few minutes in the morning with healthy food and beverages is a great routine to start immediately if you don't already do this.

Meditate. If you do the Rodney Yee AM yoga session, then he adds about 3 minutes of meditation at the end. And, surprisingly 3 minutes of meditation a day can provide amazing benefits. My qi gong teacher told me that meditating a few minutes every day is more beneficial than meditating for a longer period of time on the weekends. Some people teach that you need an hour of meditation a day. I disagree.

Meditation benefits us physiologically, psychologically, and spiritually.[11] I've seen lists of 100 benefits of meditation, but I'm going to share just a few of them here. It helps with respiration and blood flow, reduces anxiety, helps us relax, strengthens the immune system, increases brain electrical activity, increases serotonin to improve mood and behavior, assists with creativity, improves memory, and helps cure insomnia.

The easiest and most effective way to quiet your mind is through meditation. Meditation is simple – it means sitting still and breathing! Meditation is FREE and it has no negative side effects. I recommend you start with just 3 minutes per day. Meditating daily for 3 minutes will provide much better results than meditating for 20 minutes once a week. You can listen to meditation music, Native American flute or Mozart. Or, you can sit in silence if you have a place to do so.

As we wrap up this chapter, I want to make a few simple suggestions for creating an evening routine. Especially when we've lost someone who shared our household, having a calming evening routine can help to fill the void we feel without that person. The things in this evening routine list can assist you with calming down, releasing negative energy, and preparing to sleep soundly.

Take a shower before bed. Most Americans are taught to bathe and shower in the morning, washing our bodies at night is the best because it helps us to release any stress or negative energy from our day. If you are a caregiver or health practitioner, this practice will change your life and the timing is important.

Take an Epsom salt bath. A couple of times a week or right after a massage or energetic therapy session, I highly recommend you do this to clear out the energetic cobwebs. Add one cup of Epsom salt and a few tablespoons of baking powder to a very warm bath and soak for at least 15 minutes. This will help to balance and calm you before bed.

Drink a soothing beverage. Non-alcoholic is best although if you are a person who can drink a single glass of organic wine, then that is ok, too. It is helpful to find an organic herbal tea or herbal tea mixture that doesn't give you nightmares. I like peppermint. Some people like chamomile. I also enjoy a ginger turmeric tea especially if I'm feeling physical pain or strain.

Write in your gratitude journal. This is a small thing that generates big results. It is a way to focus your mind on what you've accomplished during the day and staying positive. You can also set the intention to sleep soundly and wake up refreshed and ready to start tomorrow with new energy and optimism.

Turn off electronics at least half an hour before bedtime. Put your phone on Do Not Disturb (you can actually allow certain people to override this in case of emergency). Do not have a television in the bedroom. Don't check email. Take time for yourself. If you want to read an uplifting book on an electronic device, turn it off a few minutes before sleeping and listen to some soothing music or meditate for a few minutes.

So, we've now provided quite a bit of information about rearranging your schedule and infrastructure to create a solid foundation for healing. Don't feel like you have to do all of the things we suggested here. I recommend you pick and choose a few things from each list and try those and see how they work for you.

Now, it's time to explore some ways to help us focus on the realities of living after loss that will make us feel more stable, balanced, and positive.

Chapter 8

Discovering a New Perspective

"Sometimes the hardest person to walk away from is the person you always assumed you were."

- J. M. Storm

Hopefully now you feel as though you are getting your feet back under you, obtaining the assistance you need from others to manage the logistics of your life, and have created some new morning and evening routines to help you feel calmer and more balanced.

This next exercise might just be the most important one that any grieving person can do. I've never heard any grief guru or psychologist or actually anyone talk about it; but for me, it was an essential exercise that I needed to do after my brain injury and after other losses in my life so that I could keep myself from going into deep depression, to feel more confident, and to continue to move forward.

As an example, let's just assume that you have lost your spouse. And the new reality is that you are not going to have that person in your life, in your home, in your bed, nor by your side physically ever again. And, this really can be derailing. When our entire lives and our entire identities and our primary support systems are so integrated with the life of another person, then losing that person can make us feel as if we are nowhere. We can't imagine our lives going forward. We also don't know how we will ever enjoy our lives again.

It is interesting to me, and I've learned this from working with so many people whose spouses have died – that it doesn't really matter if your spouse was your soul partner, or if your marriage was happy, or if you even liked that person. When a spouse dies - the result is total and complete devastation. Dealing with radical change is difficult for everyone. And losing a spouse has so many implications for daily living and the future.

I wrote about this extensively in my book *Stress Free Success,* how American society values marriage and expects people to be married. And, then I did the research and determined that one third of Americans live alone. So, the concept of thinking that is best to be married and that married people are better people who are more emotionally functional and lucky to have found a loving relationship – is not totally true. And, when you look at the divorce rate, we know that not all marriages are happy.

It is so easy in our society to define ourselves as being part of a couple, as Joe's wife or Cheryl's husband. And, people who lose spouses have a tendency to only remember the good times, especially in the beginning, and make the loss the central them of their lives going forward. This is really normal and actually what most Americans do.

And, at some point surviving spouses must deal with all of the integrated infrastructure stuff– like finances, property ownership, home maintenance, family obligations, mutual friends, pets, etc. But initially, we need to start by figuring out how to cope with the reality of going to bed every night and waking up every morning without that person. Regardless of your situation before, your situation now is most likely terrifying and very, very overwhelming.

So, where do we go from here? I really am an advocate of just ripping the bandage off and starting fresh as soon as is humanly possible. And, as soon as you can take this first simple step, and it might feel like a big one, then everything else that follows will improve. I promise.

The decision to accept the reality that your life is what it is will release a big part of the burden of grief. You can no longer identify yourself as your partner's spouse, as married, as part of a couple. You are now you. And you have a whole lot of life in front of you.

It is time to create a new definition of success. How we define success is fundamental to how we see ourselves and if we think of ourselves as good or bad, fortunate or unfortunate, weak or strong, and as winners or losers. Most of the time, we create our definitions of success by starting with a checklist in our twenties and we believe that if we complete each item in a linear fashion at the proper time, then we will be successful.

But, in reality, life is a moving picture and not a snapshot. Things happen every day that influence our abilities to achieve our visions of success. And, as we become older and wiser, we realize that the definition of success changes constantly.

Traditional American society tells us that successful people graduate from college and marry their college sweethearts (someone of the same race and opposite gender) and then get good jobs, buy a home, have a couple of kids, etc. etc. But life doesn't work that way. Not every successful person graduates from college (have you ever heard of Bill Gates?). Not everyone wants a partner of the opposite gender. Some of us are just born to be nomadic explorers and owning a home is a huge burden. Having kids isn't for everyone.

So, one of the most significant things I've learned, especially in the twenty one years since my life took a big huge detour after my brain injury, is that the only person who can genuinely determine how successful I am – is me. And, also my definition will be adjusted as my life journey and circumstances evolve. And the only person who can determine what makes my life the very best it can be and what works for me – is me. And, this is also true for you and your life.

But, before we move on, I want to revisit a myth about death and dying that we talked about earlier. How much we suffer after losing a loved one is not necessarily representative of how much we loved them. How much people suffer and how much they loved someone are two very separate things. Yet, most of us feel as though our misery honors and pays tribute to our departed people. And, this is simply not true.

Suffering is debilitating. And it can create all sorts of havoc in your body, mind and spirit. So, at the end of the day, you are in control. How much you choose to suffer, and how quickly you choose to rediscover happiness and how easy it will be for you to build a new, positive life – is really all up to you.

So, now let's talk about where you are right now. Are you ready to look at your life and re-evaluate your definition of success? If you just take a leap of faith and do the following exercise, I believe that it will help you to re-frame your situation and take a great big step forward on your healing journey.

Here's a quiz to help determine how you define success today and how your definition may be evolving.

1. What expectations did you have for your life before you faced the challenges you are dealing with now?

2. How did you define success before tragedy struck or you began to feel stuck?

3. What elements of that definition do not serve you in your current situation?

4. What pressures are you feeling from others? Medical professionals? Family members? Friends? Colleagues?

5. Which of those pressures don't feel right to you?

6. Which of the answers to question 5 are you ready to release now?

7. What is your new near term definition of success (what things will make you feel better when you allow them to happen)?

8. Without editing, quickly list the qualities you admire about three people you respect and what you appreciate most about those people.

Take the time now to write your own personal list of things that define success in your life – the ones that are true to you and free you from limiting expectations of others. Bonus: Review your answers from question 8 and realize that the answers you listed are qualities you possess!

Congratulations on having the courage and taking the time to think about these questions. You may find over time that your answers change and that your definition of success changes, also. It's all good. By completing this exercise, you are on your way to redefining your perspective about your loss and beginning to focus on what you learned, what you gained, and what you desire going forward.

Now, since you bravely and successfully completed the last challenge, let's dig a little deeper and do some serious healing. Again, through my work as a medium, I've discovered that most survivors feel angry and/or guilty after someone dies. They may be looking for someone to blame, especially if their loved one died by being hit by a drunk driver, or because of a medical error, or through suicide, or in an act of violence. Those who remain might also feel guilty themselves about what was said or left unsaid, or by things they did or didn't do before, during, or after their person crossed over.

Carrying the burdens of anger and guilt create those bad, destructive, disruptive, suffering vibes we talked about. And those vibes percolate and fester and dig in deeper and deeper over time. Eliminating those vibes is one of our primary goals.

And one of the most effective ways to detoxify mentally, physically and energetically is to forgive. We need to forgive the person or people who may appear to have been responsible for our loved one's passing. Remember, we've already determined that the soul decides and that when someone dies, it is never anyone's fault.

We may need to forgive the person who crossed over for leaving us alone or leaving us to face big challenges in our lives. And, most importantly, we may need to forgive ourselves.

We may need to forgive ourselves for thoughts, actions, feelings, decisions, procrastination, and for a huge long list of other things we regret. When we forgive, we heal; and when we let go, we grow. I've seen this quote many times, but never found the source, so I modified it slightly and included it here. Thank you to the person who first created it.

The process we will use to forgive is the Hawaiian practice called Ho'oponopono. It has been used for centuries in Hawaii and Polynesia. It is simple. And it works.

First, get a pencil and paper and hand write a list of all of the people related to your loved one's passing that are causing you resentment. The list can include your departed loved one, family members, friends, professionals who may be involved in assisting you, and finally, yourself. Choose a time to do the exercise when you can relax afterwards.

If you have a special location that is private and makes you feel calmer, you can do this exercise there. But, just make sure you are in a place in which you won't be disturbed.

Now, take three, deep cleansing breaths – in through the nose and out through the mouth. Center yourself in a place of calmness.

For each name on the list, say the following out loud.

[Person's name]

I love you.

I'm sorry. [If you want to expand on this, you can say all of the things for which you are sorry.]

Please forgive me.

Thank you.

Please breathe through the exercise and if they happen, then feel free to release your burden through crying as many tears as you need and clearing out the grief in your lungs by coughing.

When you have finished the exercise, take three more cleansing breaths.

Depending on the length of your list and the amount of challenge you feel for each name, you may want to do one name at a time over a number of days, or a few names each day, or if your list is short, you can complete the entire list in one sitting.

When you have finished with the list of other people, do this exercise for yourself.

[Your name]

I love you.

I'm sorry. [If you want to expand on this, you can say all of the things for which you are sorry.]

Please forgive me.

Thank you.

When you have finished going through your list, you can take an Epsom salt bath or schedule energetic or massage therapy to help complete the release process.

You can use this exercise throughout your life whenever you feel overwhelmed, stressed or angry. This exercise will set you free.

I'm really proud of you because you are still reading this book and you are taking the time to complete the exercises. When we make a decision (it has the same three letters "cis" as the word "scissors" and implies cutting away or removing something), then we demonstrate that decision by taking action to welcome what we desire and release that which no longer serves us.

Chapter 9

Becoming Stronger

"Don't worry. Be happy."
~ Bobby McFerrin

It is really exciting how we've progressed on our journey
and have gotten to this point. Hopefully you have created
daily routines that work for you and are benefitting from
them in your daily live. Also, by now you should be
moving forward by benefiting from the assistance of
others. Because you have created a new, energetic
foundation by seeking therapies that work and shifting
your perspective; you should start feeling more positive
and motivated.

Now, it is time to talk about making your body stronger
and more stress resilient because grieving can deplete our
health and physical strength. Grief settles in the lungs, so

if you have been struggling with bronchitis or having a persistent cough, this is normal. Energy healing and therapies that release tension will help with this. If you have a persistent cough that lingers for weeks, you may want to seek medical attention.

When I talk about the body, I do it from a holistic perspective that is based on Eastern philosophy and healing modalities. If you aren't familiar with this approach, don't worry. This will just help you create a new framework from which to think about your physical body and healing.

Many of the things we are going to talk about in this chapter start with the assumption that our bodies are naturally, self-healing ecosystems. Imagine that your body is like a lake. If you poured chemicals into that lake, then the ecosystem would become polluted and toxic. Plants, fish, and other species that live in the lake and surrounding environment, such as birds and other wildlife – would eventually become ill and some might even die.

Avoiding exposure to chemicals in your day-to-day life is one of the best things you can do to make your body stronger so you can overcome mental, physical and emotional pain and suffering. We need to be aware of how we are exposed to chemicals through our environment and lifestyle choices we make. We also need to know that we ingest chemicals through our skin, what we eat and drink, and through exposure to things like household cleaning products, lawn chemicals and fertilizers, and environmental pollution.

Making your body more resilient will help you feel stronger physically, mentally and emotionally and increase the vital force energy of your soul.

While physical exercise increases muscular strength and overall health and wellbeing, people who are physically fit are not necessarily resilient to stress and other lifestyle and environmental factors that drain energy.

Even if you are extremely physically fit, that is only one part of the equation. In order to heal from grief, your body needs to be a balanced ecosystem in which positive energy can grow and thrive.

Reducing chemical exposure not only includes being aware of what touches our skin, what we eat and drink, and where we are exposed to chemicals in the household and office, but to also be aware of other lifestyle choices in which we unknowingly ingest chemicals.

Some of the most important things you can do to reduce chemical exposure for you and members of your family include: 1) stop drinking diet soda (it's molecular makeup resembles formaldehyde and methanol and aspartame is toxic (you can do your own research); 2) reassess prescription drug usage and be aware of drug interactions (visit a naturopath if you need assistance with this); 3) wash your sheets and linens in chemical-free laundry detergent and never dry clean bed linens; 4) do not treat your lawn with chemicals; 5) store leftovers in glass containers; 6) do not drink beverages (especially hot ones) out of Styrofoam containers; 7) reduce the number of clothes in your wardrobe that require dry cleaning or use chemical free dry cleaners; 8) only use bed linens and throws that are washable; 9) avoid cigarette smoking; 10) minimize consumption of processed foods, and 11) use glass or aluminum water bottles and minimize consumption of water out of plastic bottles. If you do drink water in plastic bottles, avoid storing those bottles in a hot car; 12) make your home a shoe-free zone; 13) wash your face, body and hair with organic, chemical free products; and 14) eat as many non-GMO, organic, non-processed foods as possible.

When I was in my early thirties, one of my best friends had a sister with a PhD in Chemistry. And, one day my friend's sister and I were having a conversation about pollutants in our environment. She told me that the single most toxic substance known to man was diet soda. She said that the chemical makeup of diet soda resembles methane and formaldehyde fundamentally, but when soda is exposed to heat (and this happens many times during the shipping and storage), the final product is lethal.

It is interesting that I could never stand the taste or smell of diet soda, so it wasn't an issue for me. But, whenever I coach clients or teach, I always tell people that if they consume diet soda, eliminating it is the first thing that they should do to be healthier. And, if I am having lunch with a friend and they order a diet soda, I try to talk them into having iced tea or sparkling water instead.

If you consume diet soda, here are some other things you can try to replace it. You can have sparkling water with lemon or lime, iced tea, herbal tea, organic coffee or clean water. The other thing you should know is that diet soda actually promotes weight gain through inflammation, not weight loss. Get it out of your life and do it now! As a general rule, you should never have soft drinks or soda pop in your home. You and your family will either be ingesting addictive sugar or toxic chemicals and both of them decrease physical strength and stress resilience.

Now I am going to get on my prescription drug soap box and will try not to sound evangelistic or preachy. Prescription drugs are risky for many reasons. They are created in laboratories. They are artificial. They also treat symptoms and not the root causes of illness. Sometimes, people are dependent on prescription insulin or thyroid medication and have no choice. But, if you do have a choice, please consider herbal or homeopathic alternatives. And, if you take prescription drugs, try to take the fewest possible because interactions between drugs cause the most risk and aren't always tested.

It is safe to say that I have a big mental bias against prescriptions because of what doctors recommended for me after my brain injury. Most people my age are taking five or six or seven prescription drugs. And, I am not taking any. For many years I did consulting in the healthcare insurance industry and was shown the realities of the financial kickbacks to insurance companies and physicians from big pharma.

I don't even have an over-the-counter painkiller in my house. Let me say here, however, that if I had an infection, I would take antibiotics. Whenever I experience overwhelming pain or emotional loss, I turn to energetic therapies.

Most of us don't even think about this, but our skin is the largest organ in our bodies. Many of us were raised thinking that washing our clothes and sheets and towels in products made by Proctor & Gamble that come in bright boxes and are fragrant, was the best thing we could do to keep things clean. And, yes, the chemicals in those products really make clothes and linens look really clean.

But, in reality, we ingest those chemicals through our skin and breathe them in on our pillow cases. Over time, these chemicals build up in the body. In the past, many of the chemical-free laundry detergents just simply didn't get things clean, but now there are so many great products on the market. Choosing chemically free laundry detergents and home cleaning products are a few simple things you can do now to increase your body's stress resilience and lessen your exposure to chemicals.

When you were a kid, did you ever hear about dogs getting cancer? And now it seems like it is becoming more prevalent. I think that dogs get cancer because of exposure to chemically treated lawns. When I lived in the Midwest, on a cul-de-sac, in a neighborhood, I had my lawn chemically treated and fertilized. But, when we do that, we expose ourselves, our kids and our dogs to harsh and toxic chemicals.

If you have a lawn and live in an environment that requires you to keep it beautiful and weed free, do the research so you can minimize the number of toxic chemicals you use. You can also modify your landscaping and reduce the amount of green grass on your property.

This will also reduce your water consumption and create a win/win scenario for the planet.

Now, we need to have a chat about plastic. Plastic, especially when heated, leaks chemicals into whatever is stored in the container. I don't remember the last time I stored leftovers in plastic. It is surprising how affordable glass containers are for food storage. Avoid using plastic containers to store food or beverages and use glass instead. Minimize microwaving (this is another entire conversation) because it alters the energy of your food and also is able to release energy altering waves into your environment.

If you do choose to microwave, never do it in plastic containers and don't heat food that is packaged in plastic bags or containers in the original packaging. If you are addicted to your microwave, try substituting it with a toaster oven. They work well and the food tastes better.

Also, invest in a good glass water bottle with a silicone sleeve to prevent it from breaking, or if you prefer aluminum that is ok too. Avoid drinking water from plastic bottles, and if you need to do so, never leave them in your car. I love that many airports now offer purified water stations for water bottle refills. Plastic pollutes our bodies and our environment. When you start to recognize this, you'll probably be amazed as I was at how much plastic you have in your home.

Another way we expose ourselves to chemicals is by dry cleaning clothes and bed linens. If possible, start buying clothes and bed linens that are machine washable. If you do need to have your clothing dry cleaned, try to find a dry cleaning shop that cleans without chemicals.

We also know that cigarette smoking causes cancer and other health issues. And, I feel like I need to comment on vaping in this book because the practice is becoming socially acceptable and prevalent, especially among the younger generation. Vaping and artificial cigarettes release foreign agents and chemicals into the lungs. If you are going to smoke marijuana (and if it is organic and used appropriately it can be very healing for people), use a glass pipe and not a vape.

Finally, and this is a really big one. Remove your shoes when you come home and don't wear shoes in your home. I was lucky enough to experience this when I lived with a Chinese family in Santa Monica about twenty five years ago. And, to this day, I refuse to wear shoes in my home or anyone else's home.

Just think about it. Think about all of the germs that are on the bottom of people's shoes. In parking lots, office buildings, grocery stores, public transportation, etc. etc. By not wearing the same footwear inside your house that was worn outside of your house – you reduce the number of germs and pollutants in a huge way.

I actually throw all of my shoes in a big ottoman bench that is by my front door. You can also buy shoe racks and put them next to the entrances to your home. In the winter, I wear slippers and I have one pair for upstairs and another pair for downstairs so I don't wear them on the stairs and fall down and break my neck.

Sometimes I wear socks or fleece socks in the winter. And in the summer, I go barefoot in my house and even in the healing center. If you were to visit me for a session in the summer in Santa Fe, I would be barefoot. Hey, anything they do regularly in Hawaii works for me.

It is also something I needed to get used to, but I also ask everyone who visits my home and my healing center to remove their shoes. If this is difficult for you, you can also buy disposable or washable shoe covers and offer them to people. If someone walks on my floors with shoes, I wash the floors immediately afterwards. I don't have carpeting in my home, so this is easy.

Not sure if we spelled this out earlier – but using chemicals to clean our homes, dishes, etc. also creates chemical exposure and there are so many great products on the market today that do as good of a job as chemical products. White vinegar works well. I personally love Grove products, especially their all-purpose cleaner concentrate (and it comes with a glass bottle). And their bamboo toilet paper is sustainable, strong and soft.

The hygiene products we choose can also influence our exposure to chemicals. Cleaning hair, body, and teeth with low-chemical products and also using organic facial skincare products and makeup are something to consider. Chemical exposure is a cumulative thing, and every lifestyle choice we make can influence our health. Fortunately so many great products are available and the marketplace is growing.

Finally, let's talk about food. Avoiding sugar, preservatives and pollutants in our food choices is important. Look for non-GMO food products, and try to minimize eating processed foods especially cereal, crackers, chips, and anything made with white sugar and white flour. I think that our food supply has changed so much in the last thirty years, and that many of these changes have created conditions such as ADHD and OCD. Read labels and don't eat anything with ingredients you can't pronounce. Also, here's a list of fruits and vegetables that you should buy organic whenever possible.[12]

- Apples

- Strawberries

- Blueberries

- Grapes

- Peaches

- Nectarines

- Spinach

- Celery

- Sweet bell peppers

- Hot peppers

- Cucumbers

- Cherry tomatoes

- Snap peas

- Potatoes

Chemicals pollute our bodies – our self-healing ecosystems. When we ingest toxic chemicals, then the body's focus is on minimizing the damage from the pollutants and this creates imbalance and potentially illness. When you minimize the amount of chemicals that you ingest and are exposed to, then you empower your body to heal itself naturally.

Chapter 10

Taking Care of Yourself

"I am not what happened to me.
I am what I choose to become."
~ Carl Jung

Another one of the essential elements to empowering your body and becoming stronger and more resilient is learning how to manage stress. Reducing stress is fundamental to feeling balanced, strong and energetic. Adjusting to life after loss creates stress on many levels – mental, physical and emotional. And stress drains energy.

Several years ago when I wrote a book called *Stress Free Success*, I invented a concept called the stress profile. The stress profile is made up of two different things. The first one is what stresses people out. The second component is what releases stress and calms them down. Each person has a unique stress profile because what stresses out one person calms another.

I think that one of the best ways to reduce stress within your household is to understand and honor the stress profiles of everyone who lives there, including pets. An example of an activity that stresses out some people and calms others is rock climbing. I personally would melt down and be terrified if I had to go rock climbing, but for some people, it is a favorite calming activity.

Some of the things that determine what stresses a person out are personality type, preferred learning modality, and upbringing. When we look at personality types, I prefer to use the method developed by Carl Jung and then packaged as the Myers-Briggs personality type indicator MBTI. Dr. Jung determined that humans show personality preferences as infants and that these preferences logically group into four different categories.

The first category is how we rejuvenate; by spending time alone or in small groups or by socializing with large groups of people. The second category is based on how we prefer to interact with the world around us and make decisions; through our five senses or by relying more on our sixth sense. The third category recognizes that we all process information differently; by thinking or feeling. And, finally we all have preferred methods of managing our day-to-day responsibilities and lifestyles; either spontaneously or by planning. You can determine your personality type by visiting truity.com and taking their free test.

Let's talk about how personality types can create or relieve stress in a typical household. Let's say that your spouse or life partner is very social, loves to entertain large groups of people and loves to attend events with big crowds such as sporting events and concerts. And, let's say that you are more of a private person and after a tough week, you'd prefer some alone time or maybe just a dinner at home with your partner.

If you understand how each of you recharges your energy, then you can learn to encourage, respect, and compromise. This particular couple would probably benefit from engaging in activities separately from time to time. The first person in this scenario hates to be alone and loves being with people. The second person is drained by large crowds and loves spending quiet time alone. This is an example in which large groups of people energize one partner and drain another.

As soon as we understand this element of the personalities of everyone in our household, we can honor and respect what each person needs.

If you are more social and extroverted and you've just lost your spouse, you probably don't like spending time alone and often feel lonely. So, it is important for you to have not just a few people to support you, but several different groups. On the other hand, if you are more of a private, introverted person, then you may find that you tend to become reclusive when you are feeling sad. It is ok to spend time alone, but you should make sure that you have one or two friends with whom you socialize so that you don't isolate yourself completely.

When we understand our personality types, we can also explain our choices to other people. If you are introverted and feeling overwhelmed, you can explain to your extroverted best friend why you won't accept her invitation to attend Thanksgiving at her house where she will be hosting forty people. It's nothing personal; it's just that being in large groups drains your energy and you need to take care of yourself right now.

The second thing that causes stress for most people is their primary learning styles. People learn in the following ways: visual people like to see things; pictures, maps, drawings and written words. Auditory learners like to hear things, remember what people say to them, and often prefer to study or work or learn something new when listening to music. Kinesthetic learners are experiential learners who want to touch things and they also learn through movement and have trouble sitting still for long periods of time. Most of us learn through a combination of these methods, but also have primary preferences.

So, if you are a visual person, then you probably love living in a home with natural light, minimal window treatments and neutral colors on the walls. You can become overloaded by too much stuff in a room. If you are auditory, then you might prefer studying with background noise because it calms rather than distracting you. You also might love audio books and listening to music when you are driving. And if you are kinesthetic, you appreciate textures and are selective about fabrics and also may be able to sort things out in your life while taking a walk or jogging or during a workout.

Let's look at how learning types could cause or release stress for someone who was trying to drive to an unknown location. Many visual learners are stressed out by too much noise or trying to remember spoken directions and would prefer to see a map while auditory learners love sound and may prefer someone to give them directions and talk them through the route. While a kinesthetic person might just get in the car and start driving, and will learn where something is by physically going there or by figuring out where the new place is located in relation to somewhere they've already been.

You can determine your preferred learning style by thinking about what you needed in school. Did you sit in the front row or on the end to make sure you could see the teacher and the blackboard? Then you are probably visual. Were you ok with sitting in the back so you weren't distracted by noise behind you so that you could hear the lecture and concentrate? You are probably an auditory learner. Are you that person who loved working with your hands in auto shop or doing woodworking or building things? Then you are probably a kinesthetic learner.

Understanding learning style preferences can help reduce stress for you and those in your household. When possible create an environment and participate in activities during your grieving journey that make you feel calm and reduce stress.

Finally, for most of us, stress triggers were programmed into us as children. In my household, doing something stupid was highly discouraged. So, I am triggered whenever I feel that I've made a bad decision and not behaving intelligently. I also feel uncomfortable when someone else's behavior makes me feel dumb.

Also, in our household, we were taught not to bother other people. When my father came home, he actually sat in a specific place at the end of the couch and no one else was allowed to sit there. We weren't allowed to talk when he came home unless we were spoken to. I sometimes feel apprehensive when I need to ask for help or for a favor. During a healing journey, understanding triggers from our childhoods is helpful because sometimes we need to overcome those in order to move forward.

Finally, I was raised in a household full of screamers. And, to this day, I can't bear being screamed at. I also have a hard time with people who react physically when they are angry by hitting things and pounding on tables.

Understanding stress triggers and calming activities and spending time doing things that reduce and release stress are valuable tools for surviving the grieving journey.

Even though each of us has a unique stress profile, there are certain activities that reduce and release stress for everyone. I encourage you to incorporate as many of these as you are able, even if you do one at a time, into your lifestyle because each one of them makes a huge difference in creating balance and calmness.

De-clutter your physical environment. Everything is energy and every object in your home, your office, and your car generates its own unique energy. By limiting the amount of stuff you have surrounding you, you will feel calmer and less harried. I recommend that everyone de-clutter periodically. You can sell, donate, discard or give away whatever you don't need. If you have challenges with this, ask a friend or family member to help you. Prioritize by de-cluttering the spaces in which you spend the most time – your bedroom, bathroom, and kitchen.

If you have lost a loved one that lived with you, determining what to do with their possessions and when to do so can be extremely stressful. Here are some things to consider. Your departed loved one no longer has any attachment to any of those possessions nor to your home. Whenever I speak with the departed in medium readings, one of the things they ask most often is for their surviving loved one to take down the shrine.

Many times when someone dies, people create memorial spaces in their homes with lots of pictures and possessions. I suggest that you keep five or six things that bring fond memories to you of your loved one, but displaying too many pictures of them can actually impede your healing journey because it encourages you to live in the past and focus on what you lost. Also, realize that you now have the freedom to discard things that you didn't like. If you hated your late husband's recliner, then give it to Good Will. If you disagreed about decorating your home, it might be a good time to paint the walls colors you like and buy new bedding in colors you love.

Also, the question often comes up, especially from those who have lost spouses, whether it is ok for them to sell the home they shared. Many times, the survivors want to move to another town where they have a stronger support system or they need to sell the house because the responsibility of caring for it alone is overwhelming. Many times, selling the home is a financial necessity. I can honestly say that every time this question is raised, the departed loved one encourages their person to sell the house and move on.

Spend time in beautiful places. Walking in nature is great, but even if you live in a city, visiting a park or garden or pond can help you release stress. It is important to have sanctuaries located in your home, in your city or town, and in your state. I love cathedrals and art museums and botanical gardens. What do you love? Spend more time there.

Meditate and pray. Calming your mind and finding comfort from a higher power are extremely beneficial to everyone.

Spend time with animals. You may have heard of equine therapy. It can be extremely effective. If you aren't an animal person or don't have pets, you can go to the ocean or the mountains and observe wildlife. Or you can visit friends or family members and play with their dogs and cats. You may even want to get a pet goldfish or a kitten to keep you company. Scientific studies have shown that animals bring tremendous comfort to people.

Laugh. Watching a funny movie, hanging out with fun friends, reading funny books and watching comedic shows or movies really helps. Many of my clients have said that they feel guilty whenever they feel happy or joyful after someone dies. We've alluded to this many times already, but guilt is an emotion that is best abandoned when we are grieving. Your departed loved ones in spirit are at peace and they want you to be, also. Suffering over the loss of your loved one, while it is normal to a certain extent – is not serving them. They want to you to be happy.

Schedule a reading with a medium: Mediums are people who are able to communicate with the departed. Every single person on earth should have a medium reading. We are all grieving over the loss of someone. Mediumship is like sex. If I explained sex to you and you had no sexual experience – you would never want to do it. Most of us can't wrap our brains around Mediumship and how it works. It isn't scary or weird. I've been a medium for over ten years and it is a powerful and life changing healing modality.

As part of your stress profile, you also have calming activities that uniquely work for you. Some people love reading books and people watching by the pool. Others love watching sporting activities and cheering for their favorite teams. Playing music soothes other people. Outdoor hobbies such as fishing, boating, skiing, hiking, or rock climbing are calming for some people. And, some people find cleaning to be a cathartic and calming experience while others simply love to cook.

Here is a list of calming activities. You can circle the ones that work for you and write in some of your own as well. It is important for you to engage regularly in calming activities and spend time doing things that not only make you feel better – but bring you joy.

Archery, Attending church services, Baking, Boating or sailing, Camping, Cooking, Cleaning, Dancing, Drawing, Dining Out, Driving, Fishing, Gardening, Golfing, Getting a Massage, Going to a concert, Going to the gym, Going to a museum, Hiking, Jogging, Needlework, Playing video games, Playing music, Playing sports, Practicing yoga, Riding a bike, Riding a motorcycle, Rock climbing, Singing, Surfing, Sporting Events, Watching movies, Watching a play, Yoga.

Adding more calming experiences into your daily life with help you to shine your light on your journey and move forward feeling stronger, more balanced and happier.

Try to do at least one calming activity per week. Write in other activities as you discover them. Do more of these activities whenever you feel stressed or overwhelmed. Also, honor the calming activities of the members of your household.

Chapter 11
Picking up the Pieces

"The cave you fear to enter holds the treasure you seek."

~ Joseph Campbell

So, how do we move forward when our life has been completely derailed by a traumatic loss? We've talked about taking care of the fundamentals, and now I'd like to talk about really getting to the place where we clear out the rubble and start living again. And, it's not simple, but it can be easier than you think.

I didn't intend to become a trauma recovery expert. Nor did I want to learn how to recover after loss by losing everything and starting my life from scratch over nearly a dozen times. But, I have learned a few things along the way and I'm sharing them with you now to show you that no matter what you have lost, your life can and will go on and at some point, everything will be ok. Every one of these challenges I faced taught me lessons and things I needed to know to fulfill my purpose of teaching people how to thrive after loss. This chapter may be difficult to read, but I'm including because it illustrates the power of perseverance.

It is interesting that for me, loss became the norm about a year after I discovered I was a medium and came out as a psychic medium to family, friends and colleagues. It started when my family of origin decided that having a psychic medium in the family was weird and strange. In 2008, I had two living parents, two sisters and three nephews. My middle sister walked away from the family in 1996 and took her six-year old son with her after she and my mother had an argument on Thanksgiving from which we never recovered. So, when my mother's death appeared to be imminent, I called my middle sister to let her know. No one else in the family was willing to communicate with her. She sent my mom flowers in the hospital, but did not see my mother before she crossed over. I haven't seen my middle sister's son since he was six, and he is 26 now.

I essentially lost my family many years ago. At some point, I realized that it was just easier to accept and move on than to carry the guilt burden. After my mother died, my dad and youngest sister reconciled after a sixteen year war they had with each other and they are now closer than ever.

In 2009, I my highly lucrative and prestigious career as a management consultant dissolved without warning. The person who had retained me (my client) was terminated because of a political coup in a huge corporation. The next day, the Vice President who took over my client's team terminated me without notice when I had $175,000 left in a fully-funded project because I had been too close to her and he identified me as "her consultant."

I could tell when I met with him in that conference room that he had probably mutilated small animals as a child and was closeted sociopath. I really felt that. He walked me out of the building and it was the first time in sixteen years of consulting that I'd ever ended an assignment in that way. It was so devastating that I lost my confidence and because this occurred right after the economic crash, it resulted in me losing my house, my financial foundation and my credibility.

But that was just the beginning of an eight year journey fraught with disappointment, death, loss and lessons. In 2015, I attempted to launch an online stress management program after my consulting career tanked. I spent a few years before designing the online program traveling the country trying to sell it to medical institutions. But I didn't have a clear product definition and the timing was wrong because it was just after the Affordable Healthcare Act was put into effect and hospitals were cutting budgets by tens of millions of dollars. So even though my program was remarkable, many of the people with whom I spoke had no training budget.

Later that year, after failing to find a marketing partner, I decided to just build the program online and market it to individuals. The marketing was much more complicated than I had envisioned, and the program didn't sell. At the beginning of 2016, I wasn't able to afford a place to live so I put everything I owned in storage in a sleepy mountain town in Colorado but because I was so strapped financially, I elected to store everything in the non-secure facility because it was cheaper.

At the time, I thought I was going to be moving in with my boyfriend within a few months, so wasn't concerned. It turned out that he had been lying to me and never intended to move from the ranch he managed, although he did take care of my cat Stewart for 9 months while I traveled the country staying with friends and house sitting.

In the spring of 2016, I hadn't given up on the stress management program and was trying to get a meeting at Aveda to see if they would be interested in partnering with me. Even though I had potential connections, the doors kept shutting. I also had a contact that could get me into the Mayo Institute, but it turned out that they were concerned that my product would look better than theirs, so they decided not to help me. 2016 was a year that should have killed me. I can say with certainty that it was the worst year of my life.

At this point, I'd lost my family, my career, my credibility, my money, my confidence, my boyfriend, my cat, and I was separated from all of my possessions. So, what keeps us going when we are in this situation? Here are some of the things I did.

First, I had to create a new definition of success and stop defining my value to the world based on every single thing society tells us we must have to be worthy of being on the planet. I was no longer able to assess my self-worth based on my job, my income, my bank account, my zip code, the car I drive, my marital status, my home, my possessions, or most importantly, what others thought of me. I also gave up complete control because when you don't have a place to live; you end up either living as homeless person, or staying with friends. And even when those friends are supportive and doing everything they can to help; it can be very difficult.

I learned so much during those nine months when I lived with other people. My first adventure was staying in a small town in the Pacific Northwest where a friend of mine had accepted a job after finishing graduate school. For the sake of maintaining decorum, let's call my friend Lynn. Lynn's husband wasn't able to join her for three months and so she offered to let me stay with her since I didn't have a place to live. I was still doing phone readings and that was my primary income, but really didn't have much extra money and she knew this. I met Lynn at a spiritual retreat and had stayed at her house once and she and her family had stayed at mine. We talked on the phone at least once a week, but as I realized early on in our trip, I didn't know her at all.

But, I had never been to this place where she had just accepted a job, and it was really beautiful there, and I didn't have anywhere else to go; so I accepted her offer. I packed up three weeks of clothing and my inflatable bed and a few linens and she picked me up in Colorado where I had been house sitting and we loaded my things into her car and began the journey. I should have known that things were going to be precarious when she gave me the first instructions the minute we got into the car. The plan was to stay in hotels that I had found and reserved for two nights. So it would take us about two and a half days to drive to her newly rented house.

So, she said, "I just wanted to let you know how things are going to work. No one drives my car, not even my husband so you will not be driving my car. I'm not willing to stop every time you need something, so when we stop for gas you need to go to the bathroom. I will decide when we stop. Also, I have this thing about smells and scents, so please don't bring anything into the car that has a scent. I will decide where we will eat." And, that was how the trip started.

Lynn had a new vehicle and so her cell phone was integrated. We had been driving for about 6 hours or so when her phone rang and she answered it on speaker. The person on the phone was her friend who was coming to interview at the same place where Lynn had just gotten a job. We left Colorado on a Monday and Lynn was supposed to pick her friend up at the airport on Wednesday night and drive her to her interview on

Thursday morning. Evidently Lynn's friend had a fear of driving in towns she wasn't familiar with.

So, they started the conversation and then Lynn's friend said, I'm so excited to see you tomorrow night. And then Lynn said, "no, Wednesday night." And then her friend explained that her interview was Wednesday morning, not Thursday. So, now our plan changed. We were going to drive for 9 more hours, cancel our first hotel reservation and stay in the second location because Lynn had messed up the dates. In hindsight, I think Lynn only wanted to pay for one night in a hotel, but she didn't want to tell me that, and so the whole thing about mixing up the dates was rehearsed.

So, I had to scramble to cancel the first reservation and move the second one up a single day. And, now I was dealing with chronic pain from sitting in that crowded car with no way to move around (a side effect from my brain injury) and having to stay awake to talk to Lynn who was now going to drive fifteen hours straight through the night. We were traveling through Wyoming and Utah and so we were in a remote part of the country. I was sleep deprived and terrified and frustrated.

At about 1 o'clock in the morning, we were in the mountains of Utah and encountered a really scary spring snow storm. I'm from Colorado, and it was one of those storms in which the snow was coming down really hard and it was icy. Lynn's vehicle wasn't four-wheel drive and she wasn't the best at driving in those conditions. There were moments when I really wondered if I was going to die that night on a remote mountain pass in the middle of nowhere. We finally reached the hotel at about 3 o'clock in the morning and Lynn told me that we would be getting up at 6 AM sharp, having breakfast at 6:30 and then getting on the road by 6:45 so we would get to our destination in time to unpack the car so she could meet her friend at the airport that evening.

I stayed with Lynn for one month. She had promised to put some furniture in the house we were sharing, but decided after we got there that she wanted to wait and not spend the money. She had ordered a new bed and linens online and the landlords set up her bed so it was ready for her when we arrived. She furnished her bedroom with a desk and a chair and some nightstands and lamps and everything she needed for a comfortable sanctuary. All I had in my room was my inflatable bed, linens, my favorite Ralph Lauren blanket, and a duffle bag with clothes.

I spent every day in the house alone with no car, in the middle of nowhere where I couldn't even walk to a grocery store. I mostly sat on my inflatable bed or on a camping chair on the back deck that the landlords had provided. I did have an iPad and a laptop and Internet access, although the house didn't have a television or stereo. At least I was able to read online and send emails.

She also refused to give me a key to the house and our laptops were in there; so I was a prisoner because I couldn't even walk around the block because I would have to leave the house unlocked. Lynn came home every day at lunch to check on things. I'm sure this sounds as if I'm exaggerating, but seriously, this was the situation and I was powerless to change it.

At one point, Lynn and I had a conversation that nearly broke me. She had always had a real job, and didn't have an entrepreneurial bone in her body. One Saturday morning, we were talking about why I decided to start my own business in 1996 and how I had ended up in this situation. She just kept asking me questions about why I did this and why I decided to do that and why I believed certain things. Finally, she said, "Well, no wonder you are in this situation. I'd be homeless too if I quit my job."

She implied that all of my efforts to create something that would make a difference in the world were things for which I should be ashamed. She implied that I was irresponsible, lazy, and stupid. So, here I was in this house living with a sadist. She controlled my access to food because I depended on her for rides to the grocery store or restaurants, and we went only when she felt like it. Every night after I went to bed, she would take the car and go and get fast food and talk to her husband on the phone. She only left vegetables in the house because of her issue with scents. She was really selective about what could be in the refrigerator.

I was rationing food. I had no money, no place to go, and was dependent on her for a plane ticket back to Colorado. But, you know what I decided? Living with her made me realize that I really had my act together. I was a happy person. I was mentally stable. I was a survivor.

And, unlike her, I wasn't cruel and I wasn't a control freak.

While I was staying with Lynn, I'd been having weekly conversations with my friend Jeff who lived in San Francisco. He started to worry that my situation wasn't safe for me, physically or mentally. He offered to drive up and pick me up and take me to his place for a few days; and if Lynn didn't get me plane ticket back to Colorado, then he would give me one with miles.

Finally, on May 1st, 2016, my friend Jeff picked me up and took me to San Francisco and treated me like a queen for several days. I had convinced Lynn to buy the plane ticket she had promised me at the beginning of our trip, and so I was able to fly back to Denver. At first, she tried to wrangle out of our agreement by suggesting that I take a bus or a train. But, I put my foot down and told her that a deal is a deal and she had promised me a plane ticket when I first agreed to come with her. A friend picked me up at the airport, and I house sat for her for a few weeks.

During the next several months, I stayed with friends and at one point, with my middle sister. I won't go into details, but will summarize my experiences. Even though those six months in 2016 when I didn't have a home were some of the most challenging times, if not the most challenging time of my life. I learned so much about myself and other people and also about human psychology by staying in other people's homes.

At one point, I lived with a friend who had challenges with having too many possessions in her home almost to the point of living as a hoarder. So, to pay her back for staying with her; I helped her organize her life and create space within her home. Living with this challenge is extremely overwhelming and creates a monumental situation that is difficult to face and overcome. We organized her life one room and one closet and one drawer at a time.

I stayed with a closeted alcoholic who began drinking before she went to work in the morning. She asked me not to go upstairs to her bedroom while I was staying in her house, and she provided an extra car for me to use, but she also asked me not to get into her car. I realized later it was because her car reeked of wine and she had all of her alcohol stashed in her bedroom. I wasn't aware that she started drinking the minute she got out of bed in the morning. She eventually went to rehab and has now been clean and sober for several years. I applaud her courage.

After staying with these people, I went back to Colorado to house sit for a friend for two weeks while she went on vacation. I remember I was sitting in a restaurant, eating lunch before going to her house. And, my phone rang and I saw that it was my middle sister with whom I hadn't spoken for a year since our mother died and before that, for twenty years. I didn't answer my phone in the restaurant, but all of the sudden, I felt this sharp, stabbing pain in my right knee. All I did was move my leg.

And, when I stood up; I couldn't walk. I had to literally put a chair in front of me and lean on it like a walker all the way to my car. When I arrived at my friend's house, she was at work, and I had ease myself down on the ground and roll across her lawn and up onto the porch because I couldn't stand up. And, then I checked my voice mail and heard my sister's message asking me to call her back.

So, I returned my sister's call and learned that my 27-year-old nephew, my youngest sister's son, Eric - was probably dead. My middle sister's son was Eric's friend on Facebook and called her to say he had seen posts that said RIP on Eric's wall. And because my middle sister and I were both estranged from our family (for different reasons), we couldn't call anyone to find out what happened. So, we put the pieces together over several days by searching on the Internet until we found the time and place of Eric's memorial service. As I think back, the entire thing was so tragic and surreal and sad.

At the memorial service, my sister and I were sitting in the back row and I recognized two of Eric's mom's friends and former neighbors sitting in front of us. I recognized them and introduced myself. We then started talking and I asked them what happened, and they explained that Eric had taken a gun and blown his brains out. I'm not kidding.

All I could think was "thank goodness I heard about it from them, because had I learned about it during the memorial service, I might have just melted down or passed out." Several of Eric's friends spoke at the service, and it was just heartbreaking. My middle sister didn't know Eric, so she wasn't as overwhelmed with grief as I was. It was a very dark day. And, when I left the service, all I could think about was whether or not I could have prevented Eric's suicide. But the wise sage inside of me knew that the answer to that question was a definite "no."

The next week, I went see my own personal healer, David. I'm kind of picky (ok extremely selective) about who works on my energy because I'm so sensitive and because I know too much about energetic interaction. And, he has been there for me for years. David has many gifts including magic hands, incredible skills with energy healing, tremendous compassion, and a strong connection to the cosmos. He is not only an amazing healer, but he is a gifted intuitive.

The good news is; that after our session, I was able to walk much better, and I went back a few weeks later so that I could continue to strengthen my leg and eventually walk normally again. David and I both agreed that the knee pain was definitely caused by Eric's passing. It brought me to a grinding halt energetically. I think it is important here to emphasize that I didn't get an x-ray, nor go to a medical doctor, nor take a prescription painkiller. I took turmeric tablets and walked with crutches and continued my meditation and gratitude rituals. But, energetic therapy was fundamental to my recovery. It was essential.

At the end of our second session, David said to me "Ok, I just need to tell you this. So, I'm going to just say it. You need to talk to your nephew. He is here and he really wants you to talk to him." And tears welled up in my eyes and I said to David, "I'm not sure if I have the strength to do it." And David then lovingly let me know that Eric had information for me that I really needed to hear and that it would be healing for both of us.

I'd already spoken with a medium friend the minute after I heard that Eric had possibly died. I called her and she delivered messages that confirmed that Eric was on the other side and that he was ok. But, we didn't go deeply into detail right then because I was completely in shock.

After Eric's memorial service, I had a week of house sitting left, and then no place to go. I was broken physically with a knee injury. I'm clairsentient, so I feel energy through my body. I really believe that the stabbing pain I experienced in my right knee was directly caused to Eric's death. The pain was on the masculine energy side of my body and it happened when the phone rang before I even knew about the tragedy. I asked my middle sister if I could stay with her for a while. At the time, she was looking for a job, and I was able to help her with that a little bit, but she was financially challenged and very stressed out.

I ended up staying with her for three nights and that experience brought up every piece of baggage from my childhood and all of the emotional dysfunction from my family of origin. About midway into the second day, she started snapping at me for every little thing I did that stressed her out. When I left on the third day, she reprimanded me for going to live in my car and leaving her with the guilt burden of turning me away. I haven't spoken to her since. They say that healers have challenging families of origin so that we can learn compassion. And, I am one compassionate person. I have also developed an inner strength and faith that have seen me through many traumatic situations.

After leaving my sister's house in Denver, a week after Eric's memorial service and the second week of August of 2016, I returned to the mountain village of Woodland Park, Colorado to begin living in my car. I could write an entire book about what it is like to live in a car and the wisdom I received from it. Before I did it, I Googled how to live in your car and am so thankful I found this article written by this guy in Australia that taught me everything I needed to know. So, at least I had a plan.

I'm sharing this with you because I think that homelessness is so misunderstood in America. Before I experienced it myself, I had no idea what it was like and how devastating it can be. I'm also talking about this here because I want you to understand that even though I haven't lost what you have lost; I know how it feels to feel totally and completely devastated and recovering from many life-altering traumas has made me an expert at what it takes to rebuild a life after loss.

Here is a typical day of what it was like to live in my car, a 1990 Chevy Blazer. Many of the challenges started at bedtime, so we will begin there. Here's the scenario. At dusk, I would drive to a quiet street and park across from an office building my friend owned that was isolated with very little traffic and with only a few homes nearby. Overnight parking is illegal in most commercial business lots, and I selected this location very carefully. My car has tinted windows, so I would put a sun shade on the front windshield, dress in a long-sleeved T shirt and yoga pants, and sleep in the middle of a down comforter on top of a sleeping bag pad with the seat folded down in the back of the car. I taped a black trash bag with duct tape over the window that let in light from the streetlight so anyone outside the car couldn't see me.

In order to get into the back of my car, I had to open the hatchback and crawl in and then shut the hatchback from inside. My car is a two door and I would hurt my knee (still injured from when I learned that my nephew died) and every time I tried to go in through the driver's side door and wedge into the back, I would make my knee injury worse. So, I started getting into my sleeping area through the back. In order to exit, I had to shove the driver's side seat forward, and then do contortions so that I could reach around and unlock and open the door and then exit feet first into the street. It was awkward and if anyone saw me, it would probably look suspicious.

The biggest fear of sleeping in your car is being discovered by police. Living in a car is illegal in most states. And, I also never drank alcohol in case I needed to drive at a moment's notice or if the police found me and my car smelled like alcohol, I could be arrested. At the time, alcohol wasn't in my budget, but it could have relieved stress or helped me sleep. I was also worried about having a concerned citizen see me sleeping in my car or getting in and out of my sleeping space, and calling the police.

Finally, I had to limit my liquid intake so I wouldn't have to use the bathroom in the middle of the night. One night I ate something that disagreed with me and had to go to Walmart at 1 in the morning with stomach cramps. I never slept overnight at Walmart because the parking lots have really bright lights and so many people sleep there. I didn't want to be recognized, and I was concerned with being taped on a security camera or that police would look for vehicles that were there overnight on a regular basis.

Walmart is one of the few commercial parking lots that allow people to park vehicles overnight legally. If it weren't for McDonald's and Walmart, I would have never have made it through living in my car. McDonald's opens at 5:00 AM and their bathrooms are really clean and located on the side of the restaurant so you don't have to buy anything to use their restrooms. They also offer free Wi-Fi access, so I could have breakfast there and check emails.

Ok, so back to the morning scenario. If I was able to wait to use a bathroom until after 5:00 AM, then I would go to McDonalds and use their bathroom. I had stuff in my car so that I could wash my face and brush my teeth, and used disposable wipes to clean my body, so I never did that stuff in public bathrooms. If I needed a bathroom before 5:00 AM, then I would go to Walmart although it made me sad because their employees would see me there using the bathroom every day, and I could tell that they knew that I was homeless.

After the morning bathroom break, I would have breakfast, usually at McDonald's because it is inexpensive and crowded so people don't notice you. Occasionally, I used the bathroom at Safeway and bought breakfast stuff there, but one of the store managers recognized me and I think she knew I was homeless because of the way she treated me; so I never went back to Safeway in the morning again.

After breakfast, I would try to find another place to sleep before it got too hot because I would have slept poorly the night before. The other reason I'd sleep during the day is because when you live in your car, you have no place to go and sleeping helps kill time. During the day, the Walmart parking lot was actually a good choice because it is so huge and I parked at an end space at the far back of the lot where I wouldn't be disturbed.

Again, my challenge was getting into the back of the car without being seen. I would back my car into a secluded space on the end of the lot next to this retaining wall and put the sun visor on the windshield. Then I would attempt to get in and out of my sleeping space in broad daylight without being seen by anyone.

One day, I changed my overnight sleep location to a little parking area behind this Mexican restaurant, because someone was walking their dog the night before at my usual space and I sat up and saw them right next to my car and was worried that they had seen me. The part I didn't anticipate about the new location was that there was an apartment complex nearby and residents walked their dogs early in the morning and when I was getting out of the back of the car, I saw this woman with her dog and was terrified that I was almost discovered.

Finding a safe place to park my car and sleep was a daily strategic challenge. And, it wears on you. I started to realize that I couldn't relax and I didn't feel safe. I also started noticing other homeless people. I'd see them at Safeway putting food into their coolers in the trunks of their cars at 6:30 AM. I saw one elderly woman with a camper van let her little dog out and then go in for food and then come back to her vehicle. I knew she was homeless. I'd see families living in their cars at Walmart. One day, I saw a mother with three daughters in a Suburban parked at the far end of the lot and I knew they were homeless. With all of the struggles I experienced myself, I can't imagine being homeless with kids.

Now let's get back to the daily routine. Mid-morning, I would drive to a park and take a short walk (my knee was still really hurting so I didn't go far), and then I would go somewhere to get a beverage and hang out. Sometimes I would go to Starbucks and get an iced tea or go to McDonalds and use the free Wi-Fi. Living in your car can be really expensive because you have to buy food one meal at a time and you can't keep or process leftovers. I also had a space limitation so not much room to store food because I had to store bedding and clothing and water. I've never been one to eat fast food, but I ate it when I lived in the car because it was hot and inexpensive.

After getting a mid-day beverage and eating some nuts or a protein bar; I would usually go to the library. I'd sit in a chair by the fiction section and read the same book every day. I'd just take it off the shelf, read some chapters, and then put it back on the shelf and then find it again the next day and pick up where I left off. Whenever I had to change clothes, I also did it at the library bathroom because not many people go in there.

Again, I became concerned about being recorded, being seen on security cameras, or being recognized by the staff members. I read something on social media about the Colorado Springs libraries and how the patrons were complaining about all of the homeless people there. It made me feel really sad. On days when the library was closed, I had to spend most of the day in my car.

After living in my car for four days, I asked a friend if I could take a shower at her house. I went there and she and her husband invited me to stay for dinner and spend the night. It made me feel really uncomfortable and when she asked me to stay, it brought tears to my eyes. I ended up homeless not because of addiction and not because I was lazy. I invested too much of my own money in a product that failed and I was paying the price.

While I was homeless, I also pushed all of my financial resources to the limit including assistance from friends. At the time I was living in my car, some of my clients knew about it and I would often email people and ask if they needed a reading. Some did, and some didn't. It was interesting to me that some clients of mine who lived in mansions or had hundreds of thousands of dollars in the bank turned away from me when they knew that I was living in my car. Being homeless was like living in a different dimension. And, I couldn't see a way out. You can't get a job if you don't have an address. I also didn't have clothing with me that I could wear in an office.

The shame and secrecy associated with being homeless also wears on you. People judge you. As an authentic person, I found it especially difficult to hide my secret. But, every time I told someone, it became obvious that I was placing a burden on them because I could tell that they felt guilty and didn't know what to do.

On day six, I was starting to really wear down energetically from lack of sleep and poor nutrition and feeling like I had no control over anything. I saw a post on social media that one of my friends who lived in a house on ten secluded acres just outside of Woodland Park was out of town camping with her husband and their dogs for the weekend. I messaged her to ask if I could park my car in their driveway overnight for a few nights. I did this because it would relieve the burden of trying to find a safe place to park. Also, they had a gorgeous deck in the back of the house with comfy outdoor furniture, and I could spend some time there instead of at the library or sitting in my car.

She messaged me back and her response nearly knocked me over. "Don't park there. If you park in our driveway, then our neighbor will see you. He watches our place whenever we are out of town. If he sees your car in our driveway, then he will come over with his shotgun and hold you at gunpoint until the police come." Wow. I hadn't asked if I could sleep in their house. They were camping in their top of the line RV. I messaged her back and said "Thanks for letting me know. I won't go near your house."

To this day, I'm not sure why I received that response. Maybe they were afraid that I would break into their house and steal something. Maybe they felt that I was no longer reliable and they had lost all respect for me because of my situation. But this particular person had been my client and student for years. Needless to say, I was shocked and devastated and again faced with the painful reality of what happens when people find out that you are homeless.

After living in my car, I had another house sitting assignment with the same friend I'd been house sitting for all summer. Several days before I was scheduled to go back to her place, I called her. I had been living in my car for eight days and could barely walk because the pain in my knee was so excruciating from bending it every time I had to get out of my sleeping space. I was sleep-deprived and hadn't had decent food. I was losing my mind and my mojo. Thankfully, she agreed to let me come and stay with her for an extra week before she went on her vacation.

While I was house sitting and back in a house and sleeping in a bed and eating real food, the contrast between the car and that environment was so huge. I decided that something had to change or I was going to stop living as a human. I'm allergic to bee pollen so taking my own life is fairly simple. It requires some tequila, a tablespoon of bee pollen and the courage to die from suffocation when my throat constricts.

After a few nights of restful sleep and some nutrition, I realized that no one was going to save me and that I had to either save myself or die. At this point, I decided to live because I felt badly for my cat, Stewart and felt like I owed him. The last time I had visited him at my boyfriend's cabin; he picked up his favorite toy in his mouth and dropped it outside of his portable carrier. He was telling me he wanted me to take him home. It was heartbreaking.

To be honest, I had started to feel like my life had no meaning, no future, and no value. So, if I didn't have Stewart, I would have taken my own life after my house sitting assignment finished. I was so tired of the daily struggle to survive. When I hit rock bottom, I realized the only thing I had was my spiritual foundation. But, even that was starting to erode. In addition to being homeless, being suicidal is another thing that our society ignores. No one wants to hear that you are thinking about ending your life. And it is scary to tell anyone because you don't want to be institutionalized for threatening to harm yourself.

One of the things I learned that year was that we all make assumptions about people. We think that everyone else is happy and functioning well and has a good marriage and enjoys life. We don't see the struggles that people are dealing with behind the scenes. We don't see hunger. We don't see addiction. We don't see domestic violence. We don't see sexual abuse. We don't see depression. I don't make assumptions any more about people nor about their happiness or their pain. I get it. We all struggle with stuff. And, for the most, part, people don't want to acknowledge it.

After several things occurred that I won't go into here, I found a job doing intuitive readings at a spa resort in Santa Fe, New Mexico. I was able to move to Santa Fe through the grace of God and the generosity of a few people who stepped up to help.

One of my clients, whom I've never met, but who knew about my homeless situation wrote me a check for enough money to cover my first month's rent and deposit, and her only request was that I "pay it forward someday." She had lived in her car in college and really believed in the work I was doing and wanted to help me. She literally saved my life and I will be forever grateful for her generosity and genuine compassion. She was one of the few people who took my phone calls when I was homeless. I dedicated this book to her.

My friend Jeff in San Francisco also generously contributed some money so that I could move to Santa Fe. I was able to stay in AirBNB casitas until I found a place to rent with a housemate who had broken up with his partner and needed someone to share the house he was renting. It was really cosmic because he didn't want references or a credit check. He just wanted someone to share expenses. Also, most homes for rent in Santa Fe don't allow pets, or only allow dogs, or only allow cats, and my housemate had a dog. Luckily, his landlords allowed a dog and a cat.

The weekend after I moved in with him, I learned that my ex had a fight with Stewart and Stewart bit him. Stewart isn't mean, so I knew that something must have gone horribly wrong. I was able to move Stewart to New Mexico two days later, and that gave me great joy. My housemate also helped me move things from my storage unit in Colorado, one truck load at a time. We then moved together to what ended up being my dream house in the Santa Fe forest.

In 2018, I experienced the final element of loss that nearly took me down. But, again, I used my tried and true recovery protocol and got through it. We'd been living in the forest house for about a year and I still had half of my possessions in storage in Colorado. One day, late in February, I received an email that one of my two storage units had been burglarized. I emailed some friends who took pictures and put a better lock on the unit.

Thankfully, I had insurance, but sadly, every memory of my life was stolen. They took the family Bible, all of the printed photographs from my entire life, my grandmother's china, my grandfather's footlocker from World War II, my Christmas decorations, my beautiful flatware and crystal and all of the mementos I'd bought during a decade of traveling the world as a consultant. I also lost many high-end kitchen appliances including my cherished Bosch mixer.

But the tragedy wasn't over after the first break-in. When I drove to Colorado to consolidate my remaining possessions into the unit that hadn't been burglarized; I arrived to find the second unit had been burglarized as well. Fortunately, they didn't take my grandmother's rug from the 1940s, and they left my couch and chair, and didn't discover the sunburst mirror that now hangs in my healing center.

But they did take my TV and all of my table lamps, wall art that I hadn't already moved to Santa Fe. When I saw that the lock was missing from the second storage unit; I was broken and sad and felt overwhelmingly guilty. I spent several weeks beating myself up because of the guilt. I felt guilty for not putting my things in the more expensive, secure facility. I felt guilty for losing family heirlooms. I felt guilty for being in a situation in which many of my things were in storage for several years. And, I felt exhausted.

Luckily, I was able to see David in Woodland Park the day after I moved several hundred pounds of things at

9000 feet above sea level by myself into one storage unit. Without energetic therapy, I would not have been able to walk or to drive five hours back to Santa Fe. One thing I do is practice what I preach. After trauma, energetic therapy is needed to clear and release the cellular-level memory. When I returned to Santa Fe, I then scheduled a session with my energy healer here and I feel as though it saved my life because I was unable to carry the energetic burdens of loss and guilt from the latest tragedy.

In 2019, things began to get back on track. My housemate bought a house and moved into town at the beginning of the summer. And, my landlord suggested that I turn my housemate's former suite; an attached casita with a separate entrance, into a healing center and see clients here. So, that is what I did. The Quartz Trail Healing Center opened for business on June 21, 2019 on the day of the summer solstice. Clients love it because it is on sacred land and is nestled in the beautiful forest with crisp air and beautiful views.

The healing space is beautiful, and it was really interesting to me that after I moved the things that hadn't been stolen from the last storage unit in Colorado; everything I needed to live in this house and set up a healing center was there. Every single thing. I'm still amazed when I think about it. The word is starting to get out in Santa Fe about the unique type of healing I do as a medical intuitive and medium. And, I'm starting to build a healthy client base here.

During the last decade, there have been many times when I questioned how in the world I had chosen the challenges I've faced. And I wondered also how I would ever survive them. But eventually, I learned how to bounce back and now I live in a home I love with all of the treasured possessions I need and my BFF Stewart. I have new friends and new colleagues. I am also stronger than ever physically, mentally, emotionally and spiritually. And, I'm also happier than I have ever been. So, all's well that ends well.

To summarize; here are the key things I did to surviving all of the loss and crises from the last decade and hopefully they will help you, too. 1) **Live in the moment.** When I was living in my car, I only focused on what I needed to do in the next hour so that I wouldn't lose my mind. 2) **Live for the lesson.** Every setback and every loss changed who I am as a person. The lessons I learned from being homeless were priceless. I learned that I can survive anything. I learned that I am fundamentally a positive, happy person. I learned to not need possessions but to appreciate them as luxuries. I learned how to manage money and live simply. I learned to not judge anyone for any hardship they might be facing. I learned to rely on my spirit team. I learned how to ask for help and be open to receiving miracles and gifts from the Universe and others. 3) **Receive energetic therapy** and use it as your main strategy for setting up a new foundation from which to move forward. Clearing the cellular level memory of your trauma and stress is essential and fundamental to healing.

Fortunately, I learned how to transform my trauma into treasure so that I can support you in your healing journey. In the next chapter, we will share some tips and tricks you can use to use the wisdom of your loss to help others.

But, before we go there; I want to share something about my conversation with my departed nephew Eric.

Reaching out to him after my healer David told me I needed to do it was one of the most difficult things I have ever done as a medium. But after I thought about it for a while; I realized that Eric had sent a message to me through David and that I needed to respect that Spirit was working in our favor.

The first thing Eric told me was that his suicide wasn't anyone's fault. And he was really emphatic about this. He told me that no one could have prevented what happened. This is consistent with what almost every departed soul has shared with me, although Eric was the first person with whom I'd communicated who had taken his own life. He also told me that he is working with souls who also took their own lives and helping them to assimilate when they first reach the other side.

Then, Eric explained to me what happened the night he died and the circumstances that led up to the event. As soon as he shared the details with me (they ended up being too personal to disclose here), I knew for sure that there was nothing I could have done, and nothing his friends could have done, and nothing that any other person could have done to prevent his crossing over.

Eric has a great sense of humor and he also told me that the other side is awesome because he has the ability to interact with so many amazing musicians. Eric was a band promoter at one point and very into music. He also told me he was with my mom (his grandmother) and his dog, Tucker, a chocolate lab that was one of my favorite dogs ever.

I'm glad that Eric sent a message to me through David and that David had the sense to not only receive it, but to gently and lovingly suggest to me that I really must have a conversation with Eric. And, that is what great healers do. We share the tough messages with compassion and caring. Eric still checks in with me from time to time and I talk with him on occasion, and it brings me peace.

Before we move on to the final chapter, it is probably a good time to send you a message about the healing power of Mediumship. If you have never had a medium reading, then I highly recommend you get one. I do phone readings and we have some incredible mediums in the Lightwalker Beacon Healer network who also work over the phone. You can learn about them online at lightwalkerlife.com. Phone readings are equally as effective as in-person readings. If you need help finding a medium near you, then email me info@laneknows.com and I will help you find someone.

Chapter 12
Moving Forward

"When you're going through hell, keep going."

~ *Winston Churchill*

This final chapter is going to be a bit different from the previous ones because it is going to provide you with some things to think about and some questions you can answer to determine what you have learned from your trauma or loss, and how you can use that wisdom to assist others now or in the future. Depending where you are on your healing journey, then now may be a good time for you to do this; but if not, you can take a look at this chapter later.

I believe that one of the best ways to heal from anything is to give to others. Taking a proactive approach to sharing is satisfying and can help to fill the void we feel after loss.

Now, I want you to think back to your trauma and your journey thus far. If you are like me, your trauma left you with a burning desire. There's something that keeps coming back to you – it either bugs you – or it is a loose thread – or it just feels like it needs resolution. For me, it was the fact that I needed to use my brain injury to serve the world – otherwise it was just a life-destroying event. I needed my injury to be a source of empowerment for myself and others, especially people who had also suffered overwhelming trauma. What burning desire has your loss created in your life?

Also, you may have noticed that as you progress on your healing journey, some coincidences or synchronistic events have happened. Have you met people who are pivotal to your journey? Did you receive an unexpected cash infusion that can help you with your purpose?

The Japanese have a special way of mending that which is broken – by using gold to fill in the broken edges. If you look at your trauma in this way, what gold has come into your life during your healing journey? People? Wisdom? Inspiration? Strength you didn't otherwise have? Finally, what is the big AH HA from your trauma? What special gems will you take from it and how will they shape your purpose? Instead of thinking about what you have lost, it is time to focus on what you have gained.

Here are some things to think about. What is your intention going forward? What is your focus? Of all of the possibilities in front of you, where do you want to channel your energy, specifically? Finally, what is your legacy? Why were you at that place at that time on this planet to experience that trauma? What contribution can you make today that will live on when you are no longer living in your physical body?

Don't worry if the answers don't come to you immediately. Just thinking about these questions will plant the seeds that will lead you to discovering the essential elements of the contribution you want to make.

Now, let's use my own trauma recovery journey as a sample so you can understand what we are aiming for here. As I told you before, my burning desire after my brain injury was to use it to make a difference. As my journey unfolded, I discovered meditation, energy healing, and my own sixth sensory abilities. Eastern practice saved my life. My hidden treasure was Mediumship.

Discovering I could talk to dead people later in life was a real shocker, but this is the thing for which I am most grateful. Mediumship is one of the most powerful healing modalities. I always knew I had a big purpose – by big I mean one that would influence many people. My intention is compassion and this is quite a departure from my previous intention of being a respected management consultant in big corporations. My focus is transformation – not just change – but supporting profound, positive change in people.

I had three major coincidences in my journey. When power animal spirits showed up in an energetic healing session in 2007, my healer sent me to an astrologer who told me I was psychic and a spiritual teacher. This was no coincidence. In 2016, I stayed in 32 different locations to try to find a partner to take my thrive program to market. Fortunately, I didn't find one and was able to do it myself 2 years later.

And, I discovered the web tools I needed to deliver the course online – while doing marketing consulting for a realtor in 2017 – but taking that assignment gave me the tools I needed to move forward in my own purpose. Sometimes failures can be hugely beneficial to helping you fulfill your mission.

My legacy is about using metaphysical magic to influence millions and since I'm starting this endeavor at age when most people are winding down and approaching retirement, it all goes to show you that it is never too late to do that thing you are destined to do. Finally, my astrology shows three predominant strengths – entrepreneur, healer and medium. This might happen for you too – astrology and numerology help you identify your strengths and purpose by validating what you already suspect. If you've never had these readings, I also encourage you to explore them.

Now, I want you to think about the causes that you feel the most passionate about. From the list below, choose three that are most important to you.

Environmental Causes: Are you passionate about oceans, the forest, the rivers, the food supply, or global warming?

Animals: Are you passionate about domestic animals, wild animals, or sea creatures?

People: Are you passionate about caring for others by providing shelter, food, clean water, medical care? Are you passionate about children or the elderly or veterans or those in hospice care? Are you passionate about suicide prevention?

Human Rights: Are you passionate about racial equality, gender equality, or lifestyle equality?

Legal & Political: Are you passionate about crime prevention, gun control, immigration, prison reform or other legal and political issues?

Trauma Recovery: Are you passionate about addiction recovery, physical injury or impairment, the bereaved, domestic violence prevention and protection, or PTSD?

As you review the sections above, words might pop out at you or some of the words or phrases might help you think of other things about which you are passionate.

Take some time to think about your passion and then do an assessment of your personal strengths. You can identify strengths by getting an astrology or numerology reading or by just thinking about them and writing them down.

Here are some questions that can assist you in determining how you want to make a difference going forward. Are you adept at working with technology? Are you good with animals? Are you a good listener? Are you a great communicator? Are you a strong writer or artist or musician? Are you great working with kids? Are you a good public speaker or singer? Are you athletic? What are you an expert at? What do your friends tell you that you are good at? What three words define you? Passion plus strengths equals purpose.

We've just scratched the surface here in helping you determine how you want to move forward and turn your trauma into treasure. At lightwalkerlife.com, you can also take a series of online courses called the Lightwalker Thrive Program. The third course, Thrive goes into more detail and provides exercises you can do to drill down on your mission going forward.

Well, it feels to me as though we have reached the end of our journey in this book. Wherever you are in your healing process; I hope that you have found some information here that will assist you in moving forward.

Thank you for investing your time, money and energy in this book. If you feel called, please leave a raving review at Amazon. As an Indie author, I appreciate your support more than you will ever know.

And feel free to connect with me on social media or via email or schedule a time to chat at laneknows.com.

Acknowledgements

First of all, I'd like to thank Jeremy Oliver of JRo Photography, for his amazing photo of the Clark Fork River that graces the cover of this book. Jeremy is a gifted photographer and special human being. You can connect with him on Facebook at Jeremy Oliver – JRo Photography, like his page and see more of his incredible work.

I am grateful for each and every one of my clients and for their loyalty, support and referrals. Thanks also to those who helped me prove the effectiveness of the Organic Grief concept – especially Gretchen, Nicole, and Esther.

I'm also grateful to my friends who are also metaphysical practitioners who give me wise advice, support and encouragement. Some of their names are David, Chris, Kay, Heather, Edie, and Maria.

Thanks to these incredible people I've met in Santa Fe who have assisted me in moving forward on my journey. I am grateful for support from Claudia, Kristin, Erin, Luis, Carlos, Andy, Linda, Olga, Sylvie, Drew, Shama, Diane, Star, Ted, Lee, Hella, Fred, and Brendan.

Thanks to my teachers, especially Charles Virtue, Maria DeSimone, Lisa Williams, and Spring Forest Qi Gong Master Chunyi Linn. Because of their wisdom and generosity; I am able to do the work I do.

About the Author

Lane Robinson, MBA is a medical intuitive, medium, and trauma and grief recovery pioneer. She is the Chief Inspiration Officer and founder of Lightwalker, a community and online resource center dedicated to those healing from overwhelming trauma or loss. She works with clients in person in Santa Fe, New Mexico USA and conducts healing and coaching sessions via telephone.

She is the author of *Enlightened by Accident – the Awakening of a Psychic Medium* and *Stress Free Success – Where East Meets West* both available in paperback at Amazon and for Kindle.

Lane holds a Master's Degree in Business Administration from the University of Colorado at Boulder and worked as an international management consultant for over two decades. She developed a simple and effective trauma and grief recovery protocol to heal herself after a disabling traumatic brain injury and is on a mission to share this life-changing program with the world. You can learn more about Lane's services at laneknows.com and lightwalkerlife.com.

References

[1] https://en.wikipedia.org/wiki/1989_Loma_Prieta_earthquake

[2] https://www.merriam-webster.com/dictionary/soul

[3] https://www.hayhouse.com/dying-to-be-me-paperback

[4] https://www.amazon.com/s?k=proof+heaven

[5] https://www.facebook.com/theseanstephenson/

[6] https://www.youtube.com/watch?v=VaRO5-V1uK0

[7] https://www.brucelipton.com/resource/article/the-wisdom-your-cells

[8] https://hbmag.com/the-memory-in-your-cells-what-power-does-that-memory-wield/

[9] https://www.familylivingtoday.com/habits-worlds-happiest-people/

[10] https://www.youtube.com/watch?v=pxBQLFLei70

[11] https://www.finerminds.com/meditation/31-benefits-of-meditation

[12] drweil.com

Made in the USA
Las Vegas, NV
03 November 2020